✅ **W9-ABW-964**

3 9119 09013264

"Demonstrating the same range of understanding and depth
of insight displayed in his book on the Ransom trilogy, Downing here
brilliantly manages a most difficult task. . . .
An intelligent and highly readable book that succeeds in taking
the reader 'further up and further in' to Lewis's own story."
CHRISTOPHER W. MITCHELL, *director of the Marion E. Wade Center*

"An excellent and robust idea that has been skillfully and convincingly
realized. David Downing has succeeded in writing a book
that will satisfy the serious student of Lewis and also the general reader
acquainted with at least some of Lewis's writings.
I very much appreciate the elegant and sparing way that David writes and was
dazzled by the powerful speculative ending to the last chapter."
COLIN DURIEZ, *author of*
The C. S. Lewis Encyclopedia *and* The Inklings Handbook

"Dr. Downing has carefully traced the story of Lewis's conversion to Christian
discipleship as found in both published and unpublished writings.
He balances the suddenness of Lewis's final decision for Christ with the slow
maturing of mind and heart within the context of literature, myth,
and European Christian tradition. Especially valuable is Downing's discussion
of 'The Quest of Bleheris,' one of Lewis's first attempts to write fiction."
DORIS T. MYERS, *author of* C. S. Lewis in Context *and*
emeritus professor of English, University of Northern Colorado

"Here's a book that deals with the most important and neglected aspect
of C. S. Lewis's life—his conversion. Its value can't be overestimated.
It's really good—no, it's BRILLIANT."
WALTER HOOPER, *editor of*
C. S. Lewis: A Companion & Guide *and* God in the Dock

C. S. Lewis's
Journey
to Faith

THE MOST
RELUCTANT
CONVERT

DAVID C.
DOWNING

InterVarsity Press
Downers Grove, Illinois

InterVarsity Press
P.O. Box 1400, Downers Grove, IL 60515-1426
World Wide Web: www.ivpress.com
E-mail: mail@ivpress.com

Cover photograph: Hulton Archive

ISBN 0-8308-2311-5

Printed in the United States of America ∞

Library of Congress Cataloging-in-Publication Data

Downing, David C.
  The most reluctant convert: C. S. Lewis's journey to faith / David C. Downing.
    p. cm.
  Includes bibliographical references and index.
  ISBN 0-8308-2311-5 (cloth: alk. paper)
    1. Lewis, C. S. (Clive Staples), 1898-1963. I. Title

BX5199.L53 D69 2002
283'.092—dc21
[B]

                        2001051941

P	17	16	15	14	13	12	11	10	9	8	7	6	5	4	3	2	1
Y	15	14	13	12	11	10	09	08	07	06	05	04	03	02			

For my brother Don
who has been with me all the way

CONTENTS

Acknowledgments

I would like to thank first two mentors of mine at UCLA, Thomas Wortham and Georg Tennyson, who encouraged my interest in C. S. Lewis and who helped me explore the nuances of the old saying "All autobiography contains some fiction, and all fiction contains some autobiography."

I am grateful to fellow Lewis scholars who gave me the benefit of their expertise. I wish to thank especially Peter Schakel, whose knowledge, advice and painstaking editorial skill were of great assistance on this project. Bruce Edwards and Colin Duriez also read portions of the typescript and offered a great deal of useful commentary.

My colleagues at Elizabethtown College have been generous and supportive throughout the writing process. I am obliged to the Professional Development Committee for making funds available to complete my research. Thanks also to Ronald McAllister, the provost, for his encouragement, and to my fellow teachers and scholars, Paul Gottfried in political science, Louis Martin in English, Anthony Matteo in philosophy and Thomas Winpenny in history.

Research for this project has taken me a number of times to the

Marion E. Wade Center in Wheaton, Illinois, where I have always been impressed by the learning, professionalism and graciousness of its leaders and staff. Thanks especially to Christopher J. Mitchell and Marjorie L. Mead for the many ways in which they have assisted me and so many other visiting scholars. I was deeply honored to receive the Wade Center's Clyde S. Kilby Research Grant for the year 2000.

Thank you as well to Kimberly Duvall Matson, my research assistant, and to Tara Stern, my editorial assistant, for their thorough, intelligent and diligent work.

I am grateful to my agent, Giles Anderson, for his good advice in shaping the project and his good judgment about seeing it through the publication process. Mr. Anderson possesses a winning combination of professional expertise, energy, gentlemanliness and personal integrity.

I wish also to acknowledge the editorial and production teams at InterVarsity Press for their thoughtful and conscientious work. Thanks especially to senior editor Cynthia Bunch for her helpful and tactful suggestions and to the lynx-eyed copyeditor Allison Rieck. Thank you as well to Mark Smith, Kathy Burrows and Lorraine Caulton for the artful cover design and photography pages.

I count myself fortunate that members of my own family are not only among my most sympathetic readers but also among the most perceptive. Thanks to my parents, James and Morena Downing, my brother Jim and my wife, Crystal, for suggestions on clarity and readability.

I owe a special debt of gratitude to my brother Don, who carefully read several drafts of this project and offered countless valuable suggestions. Our wide-ranging discussions on every topic from salvation to semicolons have qualified him for what might be called the "spiritual editor" of this book.

Introduction

At age seventeen C. S. Lewis explained bluntly to a Christian friend he'd known since childhood, "I believe in no religion. There is absolutely no proof for any of them, and from a philosophical standpoint Christianity is not even the best."* Fifteen years later he would write to the same friend on a very different note: "Christianity is God expressing Himself through what we call 'real things,' . . . namely the actual incarnation, crucifixion, and resurrection."

This turnabout did not reflect a "Damascus road" conversion; it took Lewis all of those fifteen years to change his mind.

In fact, the brilliant young C. S. Lewis, known only for two obscure volumes of poetry, seems hardly the same person as the world famous Christian scholar, novelist and inspirational writer of later years. Just after World War I, Lewis, a wounded veteran, boasted that during his time in the trenches he "never sank so low as to pray." At about the same time he proclaimed angrily to a religious friend, "You take too many things for granted. You can't start with God. *I don't accept God!*"

---

*Source materials are listed in the notes section, arranged by page number and key words.

The wonder is not that Lewis became such an accomplished and highly regarded Christian writer; the wonder is that he became a Christian at all. The man who has been singled out for praise by Pope John Paul II as a masterful defender of the faith did not return to his own childhood faith until he was in his thirties. In his memoir, *Surprised by Joy,* Lewis describes himself on the day he got down on his knees and prayed as "the most dejected and reluctant convert in all England."

And yet what a convert he turned out to be. During World War II, his *Broadcast Talks* on BBC radio made his voice the most widely recognized in Britain after that of Winston Churchill, who offered Lewis a special medal of recognition after the war. (These talks were later collected and published as *Mere Christianity,* now considered a classic introduction to Christian faith and practice.) In the same decade Lewis's *Screwtape Letters* (1942) became an international bestseller, and he appeared on the cover of *Time* magazine (September 8, 1947).

More than a half-century later, Lewis must be acknowledged as one of the most gifted and versatile authors in the modern era. Several dozen of his books remain perpetually in print, selling six million copies a year. His prolific and wide-ranging career as a writer is nothing short of remarkable. He was one of the most distinguished literary scholars of his generation, whose works are still standard reading for graduate students in English. He was a superb storyteller as well, the creator of an award-winning science fiction trilogy and a classic children's series, the Narnia Chronicles. He is also recognized as one of the most admired and widely read Christian writers of the twentieth century, with no sign of diminishing influence in the twenty-first.

Lewis penned (literally—he never learned to type) nearly forty books in his lifetime, and another twenty collections of his essays, letters and poems have appeared posthumously. Since his death in 1963 over a hundred books have been written about Lewis and his writings. By the time the centennial of his birth was celebrated in 1998, there were four major biographies of Lewis, six collections of reminiscences, eight surveys of his fiction, with another half dozen books devoted specifically to the Chronicles of Narnia.

Already a bestselling author and a perennially popular subject for other authors, Lewis received even wider attention in the 1990s because of the play *Shadowlands,* which was first dramatized on BBC television and then made into a feature-length film starring Anthony Hopkins and Debra Winger. *Shadowlands* tells the poignant story of Lewis's later years, how he met Joy Davidman when he was in his fifties, becoming first her friend and then her husband and lover, only to lose her to cancer after three years of marriage. In this tragic loss there are haunting echoes of the other great Shadowlands ordeal in Lewis's life, the loss of his mother, also to cancer, at the age of forty-six when Lewis was nine years old.

At the time of his mother's death, young Jack was nominally Christian, but he would lose that childhood faith and not recover it again until he had reached the midpoint of his life. Lewis offered his own version of how he "passed from Atheism to Christianity" in *Surprised by Joy* (1955). But this is more an informal reminiscence than a systematic account of his pilgrimage. In this memoir Lewis focuses mostly on his childhood and schooling, then fast-forwards through his twenties to his "re-conversion" in his early thirties. His biographers have followed suit, delving into his childhood and boyhood, and then leaping ahead to his life as a Christian scholar and writer, tending to pass quickly over his teens and twenties. But many questions have remained unanswered about why one of the foremost Christian writers of the twentieth century did not rediscover the faith of his childhood until nearly halfway through his life.

The story of Lewis's arduous pilgrimage is fascinating in itself considering what a celebrated and far-reaching voice for Christian thought he has become. But Lewis's spiritual struggles go beyond biographical interest: they cast fresh light on the paths which many other pilgrims take. The worldviews he considered and the issues he grappled with are still very much with us today.

Many thoughtful seekers since Lewis's time have contemplated materialism, the view that the physical world is all there is. If that is true, then any talk of spirit, of a house not made with hands, is mere wishful thinking. Today's pilgrims are also confronted with alternative spiritual guides, the claim that occult experiments or paranormal research can provide a more "scientific" approach to spiritual life than Christian faith. Or they may be invited to affirm an impersonal Life Force, a belief which offers a generalized sense of uplift without having to commit to any creeds or commandments. So the spiritual avenues and byways Lewis explored for many years are not merely of "historical" interest. They address concerns which are still highly relevant as we enter a new millennium.

Both Lewis and his biographers have recounted his childhood in northern Ireland, his years in English boarding schools and his eventual adoption of Oxford as the place where he would live the rest of his life. This narrative seeks to trace more closely Lewis's *inward* pilgrimage: how his spiritual journey was shaped by the untimely death of his mother and a lasting estrangement from his father; by the relentless rationalism hammered into him by an influential mentor; by his early interest in the occult and the paranormal; and by the surreal violence of trench warfare in France during World War I.

Counterpoised to these influences was Lewis's ongoing quest for something he called Joy. After first seeking Joy in false guises of the erotic and the occult, Lewis increasingly began to sense a certain radiant quality in righteousness, which he discovered first in the works of George MacDonald and G. K. Chesterton, then in a circle of Christian scholars at Oxford, including most notably J. R. R. Tolkien.

A careful look at Lewis's early years reveals that he did not become an effective defender of the faith *despite* the fact that he spent so many years as an unbeliever. Rather, his Christian books are compelling precisely *because* he spent so many years as an unbeliever. He understood atheism; he felt the force of its arguments in his bones and sinews. He knew the lure of the occult; indeed, he wrote that if the wrong person had come along in his teenage years he might have ended up a sorcerer or a lunatic. And he was philosophically trained in Idealism, the assumption that some unknowable Absolute lies behind the veil of appearances. He weighed all these worldviews himself, and eventually found them wanting. So when this "reluctant convert" eventually faced up to the meaning of his Christian commitment, he entered into it with his whole heart and mind and soul.

In this account of Lewis's spiritual journey, I have generally offered a chronological narrative. Of course, a person's life does not fall into tidy sequential stages. As Lewis himself noted, a person may sometimes entertain contradictory opinions simultaneously. But attentive study of his memoir, *Surprised by Joy,* plus all available biographies and letters, both published and unpublished, reveals a clearly discernible process. Amid the ambiguities and contradictions we can trace a pilgrim's progress, even with its unscheduled sojourns, confused crossways or periods of treading in circles.

In this narrative I have sometimes set aside strict chronology, introducing passages from Lewis's later books to better illuminate how the older, Christian Lewis viewed the issues which had so preoccupied him in his teens and twenties. For example, in presenting Lewis's youthful atheism, I have quoted observations from his later books to show how Lewis the man would eventually critique the philosophical arguments and emotional attitudes of Lewis the adolescent.

Because this book's organization blends the topical with the chronological, it may be of some use to outline the chapters that follow. Chapter one recounts Lewis's comfortable childhood growing up in an upper-class Belfast neighborhood at the turn of the century, his early imaginative endeavors and his first experience of Joy, that elusive yearning for some time and place beyond human reach. This chapter also discusses the political turmoil which is so much a feature of life in northern Ireland, as well as the uncertain temper of Lewis's father and the untimely death of his mother.

Chapter two discusses Wynyard School, where Lewis was sent to join his brother soon after the death of their mother. There both boys were traumatized by a brutal schoolmaster, and there the younger Lewis developed a childhood faith, but one which was more a burden than a consolation.

Chapter three examines the period Lewis referred to as his boyhood, the years in which he lost his faith and whatever last vestiges of childhood he had retained. Lewis was a militant atheist in these years, developing a series of arguments against faith that he would later respond to perceptively in his Christian books and essays.

Chapter four presents the two-sidedness of Lewis's mind during his two and a half years of study with a private tutor, William T. Kirkpatrick, in Great Bookham, Surrey. During that time Lewis's intellect was telling him that the cosmos was a grim and meaningless place, but his imagination seemed to continue reaching out for some transcendent realm. During the Great Bookham years Lewis wrote a fascinating fragment called "The Quest of Bleheris," a tale of chivalric adventure which, perhaps unconsciously, reveals his own spiritual journey at that point in his life.

Chapter five focuses on Lewis's war experiences, his estrangement from his father and his acceptance of Mrs. Janie K. Moore as a kind of surrogate mother. Lewis's reading of Schopenhauer, confirmed by the nightmare of the trenches, created in him a sense of perpetual opposition between mind and matter, between one's consciousness and the prison house of flesh in which it seems to reside. He spent several years pondering this dualism, as seen in his early book of poems *Spirits in Bondage.*

Chapter six explores Lewis's youthful interest in spiritualism, the occult and parapsychology. In his midteens, Jack recommended to his friends several books which he felt offered "scientific" evidence that one's consciousness could survive bodily death. Increasingly, however, Lewis came to believe that these "evidences" had to be taken on faith and had little to do with his abiding quest to find the wellspring of Joy. During his first few years at Oxford, Lewis had a number of encounters with spiritualists that turned his fascination to revulsion, as can be seen in his later fiction.

Chapter seven reviews Lewis's twenties, especially his formal study of philosophy and his interest in Idealism and pantheism. Briefly summarizing the ideas of Bishop Berkeley, Henri Bergson, F. H. Bradley and others, this chapter shows what initially attracted Lewis to these thinkers and why he eventually felt the need to move beyond them.

Chapter eight traces Lewis's gradual recovery from what his brother called a "spiritual illness of long standing," ending first in an "intellectual conversion" to theism and then a more whole-souled acceptance of Christ two years later. His father's last illness and death seems to have played a part in this process, as did Lewis's deepening friendship with J. R. R. Tolkien, who provided what may have been the key paradigm shift in Lewis's spiritual journey.

The epilogue concludes with a review of Lewis's remarkable career as a Christian scholar, critic, storyteller and inspirational writer. His conversion in his early thirties helped him resolve a number of other issues he had been grappling with since boyhood: imagination versus intellect, spirit versus matter, and self-examination versus self-forgetfulness. Apart from his vast intellect, extraordinary energy and lucid writing style, the intellectual depth and broad influence of Lewis as a Christian thinker is due in part to the fact that he spent so many years as a non-Christian thinker.

ONE

THE ILL-SECURED
HAPPINESS OF CHILDHOOD

There was a boy called Eustace Clarence Scrubb, and he almost deserved it." So begins one of C. S. Lewis's best-loved stories, *The Voyage of the "Dawn Treader."* Lewis was called Clive Staples and, from an early age, he decided he didn't deserve it. At the age of four he pointed to himself and said, "He is Jacksie," refusing to answer to any other name. And so he became Jacksie, later shortened to Jack, to his friends and family the rest of his life.

The matter of choosing his own name is one of the earliest recorded incidents in Lewis's life, and it is a highly revealing one. The same boy who chose to define himself at the age of four, apart from the expectations and desires of those around him, would spend the rest of his life defining himself, and his world, differently from the conventions that he had inherited.

Lewis's brother, Warren, three years older, remembered another revelatory episode from about the same time: Jack's first encounter with the ocean during a summer holiday. According to Warren, the prospect of the Irish Sea came into view all at once, and his younger brother, then only three or four, seemed astonished and terrified when he first saw it. After a few moments of glaring hard at the ocean, however, he suddenly relaxed and soon took to the water with no further anxiety. In an unpublished memoir, Warren wrote that many years later his brother explained to him what had caused that initial shock: Jack had never seen a broad expanse of water before, and it took him a moment to master the perspective. At first, instead of seeing a sheet of water stretching off to the horizon, he had visualized the ocean as a great blue wall towering over him, like water streaming over a milldam.

This early incident seems highly characteristic of Lewis, and it is not surprising that he remembered it long into adulthood. In *Out of the Silent Planet,* the same kind of perceptual confusion occurs when Elwin Ransom first surveys the exotic landscape of Mars and fails to recognize the blue mass in front of his eyes as a lake. As the narrator explains, "You cannot see things till you know roughly what they are." In his scholarly books, Lewis took this principle a step further, arguing that Reality is not self-interpreting, that a great deal of what we see depends on who we are and what we have been taught to see. Where others had seen a Renaissance, a great rebirth, after the medieval period, Lewis offered ample evidence that civilization had never died, nor even slumbered, in the ten centuries between the fall of Rome and the rise of Humanism. Where others looked *out* at outer space and saw a black, cold void, Lewis looked *up* at the evening sky and saw the heavens, a majestic vault fretted with golden fire. One may even wonder if Lewis had that early childhood incident in mind when he wrote succinctly in *The Magician's Nephew,* "For what you see and hear depends a good deal on where you are standing: it also depends on what sort of person you are."

In the time and place of Lewis's birth, what you saw depended a great deal on who you were. Lewis was born on November 29, 1898, the second son of a successful Belfast attorney. This was the time of "the troubles" in Ireland, troubles which have yet to be resolved over a century later. Bitterness was particularly intense in the northern counties, the region known as Ulster, where British monarchs in the seventeenth century had taken over the lands of rebellious Irish earls and brought in English and Scottish settlers. Their Protestant descendants, of course, felt that they had earned their place through many generations of efficient labor, pointing out that the standard of living in Ulster had historically been much higher than in the Irish counties to the south. The Catholics, however, insisted that their ancestral lands had been confiscated, protesting that they were forced into permanent second-class citizenship by discriminatory legal codes.

Even in northern Ireland today, the terms *Protestant* and *Catholic* are at least as much political and social labels as they are religious designations. It is an ongoing conflict which not only has divided the church but has literally split the island into two nations, while also creating conflicts between social classes and neighborhoods, and within individual families.

Though the Lewis brothers were descended from Protestants on both sides of the family, one can sense the tension among their own forbears. Jack's maternal grandfather, the Reverend Thomas Hamilton, sometimes used his sermons to accuse Roman Catholics of consorting with the devil. In the meantime, his wife, Mary Warren Hamilton, hired Catholic servants in her household and supported the campaign for Irish Home Rule, which would have left the island in the hands of its Catholic majority, greatly reducing the influence of the Protestants in the northern counties.

One can see a similar pattern in the next generation, Warren and Jack's own parents. Albert Lewis was a stout Ulsterman, insisting on continued British presence and fearing what might happen if the entire island were united under a Catholic majority. At one meeting of the Anti-Home Rule Association in 1913, Albert gave an impassioned speech comparing the northern Irish Protestants to the biblical Joseph, who was despised by his kinsmen but who later provided for their rescue. By contrast, his wife, Flora, like her mother, made a habit of hiring Catholic workers for generous wages, persisting even when scrawled notes were pushed through the mail slot warning her to "send the dirty papists back to the Devil where they belong." Though she belonged to the Church of Ireland, part of the Anglican communion, Flora couldn't help but make whimsical remarks occasionally about the overzealousness of Protestant patriotic orders like the Orangemen.

Spending his first nine years in this volatile atmosphere, C. S. Lewis grew up to be perhaps the most unpolitical person ever born in Ireland. His brother, Warren, reported that during their Belfast childhood "politics and money were the chief, almost the only subjects of grown-up conversation"—an overexposure which left Jack with "a disgust and revulsion from the very idea of politics before he was out of his teens." In the copious letters and journals he wrote in his teens and twenties, Jack refers freely to every kind of literature, as well as art, music, philosophy, myth and legend, psychology, even subatomic physics. But he makes almost no mention of events that were reverberating around the world—the passing of a Home Rule bill in 1914, the Easter Rebellion in Dublin in 1916, the creation of an Irish Free State in 1920 or the civil war that followed. Jack's very silence on these matters offers eloquent support to his brother's observation that throughout his adult life Jack had little but disdain for politics and politicians.

If these early years encouraged Jack to avoid politics, they also encouraged him to avoid religion. Warren, who returned to Christianity about the same time as his brother, felt that both of them had suffered from "a deep-seated spiritual illness of long standing—an illness that had its origins in our childhood, in the dry husks of religion offered by the semi-political church-going of Ulster."

Even after he had recovered from his "spiritual illness" as an adult, Lewis's view of politics remained largely unchanged. In 1953, on setting out for a visit to Ireland, he wrote to Don Giovanni Calabria, a Roman Catholic priest in Italy, that he would never cease to love the country of his birth but that its people, both Catholic and Protestant, "knew not by what spirit they were led," that they mistook "lack of charity for zeal and mutual ignorance for orthodoxy." Lewis concluded that it is always a great mistake to confuse religion with politics, especially when the devil seems so often to choose the latter as his citadel.

In discussing his own life, Lewis tended to distance himself from "the troubles" in Ireland, stressing the Welsh origins of his father and the English origins of his mother. In his autobiographical *Surprised by Joy,* Lewis reports that he didn't remember much about his mother's religious views, which is not to say she was complacent about such matters. It seems that in the fiercely divided world of northern Ireland she was, in her own understated way, an early model for young Jack of a "mere Christian." As will be explored in chapter eight, Lewis's adult recollection of his mother's spiritual earnestness seems to have been a factor in his own recovery of the faith of his childhood.

Apart from her inclusive ideals, Florence ("Flora") Warren Hamilton also inherited an aristocratic heritage from her mother, Mary. The Warren family had been part of the landowning class in Ireland since the twelfth century and could trace their descent from a Norman knight who, as Lewis proudly notes in *Surprised by Joy*, is buried at the ancient and revered Battle Abbey in Sussex. Both Lewis brothers tended to idealize their mother's side of the family and to demean their father's. Warren Hamilton Lewis seemed especially proud of his given names. He had a lifelong fascination for the French aristocracy, and he published seven highly readable books on the political intrigues surrounding the seventeenth-century French court.

Jack was no less proud of Flora and her family, but for different reasons. In *Surprised by Joy* he draws a sharp contrast between his parents, relating the differing temperaments of his father and mother to their family histories. He calls his father's folk "true Welshmen, sentimental, passionate, and rhetorical," people who moved quickly from laughter to wrath to tenderness, but with no gift for steady contentment. In contrast, Lewis's mother's family, the Hamiltons, were "a cooler race" whose minds were "critical and ironic" and who possessed a "talent for happiness." Here the emphasis is on the Hamiltons' self-control and "coolness," a term of approval which can be found in many of Lewis's books, consistently connoting mildness, freshness and freedom from tyrannical passions. After her untimely death, Lewis would especially remember this quality in contrast to his more ebullient and mercurial father.

In his biography of Lewis, George Sayer demurs from his former mentor on this account, pointing out those anti-Catholic sermons by Flora's father and saying she herself didn't fit Lewis's characterization of the family. But the unpublished family papers collected by Warren seem to bear out Lewis's own perceptions. His father, Albert Lewis, had courted Flora Hamilton for seven years before she finally agreed to marry him. His letters to her from that period are highly effusive, almost melodramatic, with occasional bursts of passionate poetry. Flora's letters, on the other hand, are much more level-headed and practical, and on one occasion she actually upbraids Albert for being too emotional: "You know you excite yourself far too much and let yourself get miserable too easily, and it is not good for you." In general, the surviving letters between Albert and Flora bear out Lewis's sense of sharp contrast between his mother's "cheerful and tranquil affection" and his father's emotional ups and downs.

Whatever uneasiness was generated by political uncertainty or by Albert's moods, it was that "cheerful and tranquil affection" which set the tone for the Lewis household in the early years. In *Surprised by Joy* Lewis presents his early years as a nearly idyllic "childhood" at home followed by a traumatic "boyhood" in a series of boarding schools.

Critics and biographers generally speak of Lewis's early years using the terms *childhood* and *boyhood* interchangeably. This usage overlooks the more precise meaning that Lewis lent to each term. *Child* and *boy* have consistent, and contrasting, connotations, not only in *Surprised by Joy* but in all of Lewis's writings. (For Lewis, seemingly general terms often took on specific personal meanings, which he consistently applied in a variety of contexts. Those who read widely in Lewis, for example, will discover that general terms such as *cool, joy, puritan* and *magician* have special meanings in the Lewis lexicon.)

For Lewis, *childhood* referred to the years from his birth until he was nine, the year his mother died and he was sent off to school in England. These carefree years held an almost mythic status in the mind of the adult Lewis. The title of this chapter is taken from Milton's description of Adam and Eve before they were cast out of Eden: "Happy, but for so happy ill secured."

Lewis remembers his childhood home, called Little Lea, as a

place with loving parents, good food and plenty of room for outdoor play, as well as two other blessings—his nurse, Lizzie Endicott, and his older brother, Warren. He describes Lizzie with unalloyed nostalgia and affection, saying that in searching his memory of childhood he can recall no flaw in her, only "kindness, gaiety, and good sense," concluding that she was "as nearly as a human can be, simply good."

Though hardly more than a thumbnail sketch, the fond recollection of Lizzie in *Surprised by Joy* reveals that, for Lewis especially, "the child is the father to the man." Many of his lifelong attitudes were shaped in these early years. Throughout his many books, the words *nurse* and *nursery* virtually always connote that which is simple, but also that which is true and good. For example, he warns in his essay "The Poison of Subjectivism" (1943), "Unless we return to the crude and nursery-like belief in objective values, we perish." In *The Voyage of the "Dawn Treader,"* the intrepid mouse Reepicheep discovers that the nursery rhyme about the "utter East" that he learned in his cradle turns out to be quite an accurate prophecy of what to expect as one approaches Aslan's Country by sea.

We find a similar pattern in *That Hideous Strength,* where the young married couple Mark and Jane Studdock seem to be moving in opposite directions spiritually. Jane is drawn to Ransom and his company at St. Anne's, where one of the women reminds her of her childhood nurse. When her husband seeks more guidance about his new job at the National Institute of Coordinated Experiments (NICE), his supervisor answers testily, "I'm not a bucking nurse." From the metaphors alone, experienced readers of Lewis can tell which of the two Studdocks is keeping the right company.

The other blessing mentioned by Lewis—his brother, Warren—was a lifelong companion and one who helped shape the way in which Jack defined himself in relation to the world. "Warnie," or sometimes "Badger" or "Badge," and Jack spent many a rainy afternoon poring over the books in their parents' well-stocked library, delighting especially in children's stories by Edith Nesbit and Beatrix Potter, as well as tales about "knights-in-armor" and "dressed animals." They also created their own imaginary worlds of "India" and "Animal-Land," later combined into the kingdom of Boxen. Though the worlds they created seemed prosaic to Lewis as an adult, they show how much time the two spent together, content in each other's company and trying to keep as free as possible from adult interference.

Lewis does discuss one upsetting element in those early years, but the source came from within, not without. He had particularly acute nightmares and recurrent anxiety about ghosts and insects. These childhood bogeys reappear in Lewis's later books, ghosts especially representing a fear of the uncanny. In *The Problem of Pain,* for example, he contrasts the kind of anxiety one might have if told there were a tiger in the next room with the fear one might feel if told there were a ghost in the next room. In both his fiction and nonfiction, ghosts and apparitions in Lewis's books evoke a numinous dread quite distinct from the apprehension of mere physical danger.

In general, Lewis recalls his childhood years before his mother's death in terms of a happy and secure home, the simple goodness of a beloved nurse and the freedom to roam through empires of imagination with Warren. And the words *child* and *childhood,* sometimes even *childish,* carry the same connotations in all of Lewis's books—simplicity, self-forgetfulness, imagination and wonder. In *Perelandra,* Ransom's only advice to the diabolical Weston as they both face near-certain death is to "say a child's prayer if you can't say a man's." In discussing classical literature Lewis quotes approvingly a scholar who says that a child reading Homer in translation for the story may be "nearer by twenty centuries to the old Greeks" than a trained scholar, because he is "not grubbing for beauties but pressing the siege." In *The Problem of Pain* Lewis comments that, in spiritual matters, adults have no advantage over children, nor the sophisticated over the simple, explaining that even as a small child he himself had undergone "spiritual experiences as pure and as momentous as any [I] have undergone since."

Surely the pure and momentous experiences Lewis has in mind here are the recurrences of "Joy," his word for *Sehnsucht,* the longing for some lost paradise that is itself a kind of paradise to feel. In *Surprised by Joy* Lewis recalls that, one summer day when he was only six, there arose in him a memory of an earlier time when his brother had made a toy garden, bits of twigs and moss arranged in a biscuit tin. Lewis compares the momentary sensation that came with this memory to Milton's "enormous bliss" of Eden, saying that was his first experience of beauty. He adds that Warren's miniature garden, more than the actual out-of-doors, made him sense nature as "something cool, fresh, dewy, exuberant." Though he would later revel in accounts of Eden, Valhalla and Avalon, he felt that his picture of paradise always retained an element of that first encounter with Beauty in a biscuit tin.

Later, in reading Beatrix Potter's *Squirrel Nutkin,* and again when reading Longfellow's translation of Icelandic saga, the young Lewis again experienced a nameless longing, an "unsatisfied desire which is itself more desirable than any other satisfaction." In an unpublished autobiographical fragment composed about 1930, he explains more fully that it was not the narrative of Potter's book which so thrilled him, but rather the pictures of woods in their full autumn splendor. In the same text Lewis notes the unusual quality of Joy as something never quite possessed, always "over there":

the pictures in the book set him to longing for the real trees outside his house, for the robust aromas and the crisp leaves crackling
under his feet. But then walking among the actual trees in autumn
made him long for the pictures he had seen in the book.

Lewis reports a third visitation of Joy when he was reading a
Longfellow translation of Nordic myths and legends and came
across these lines:

I heard a voice that cried,
Balder the beautiful
Is dead, is dead—

Though he had no idea at the time who Balder was, these lines
filled him with the particular kind of Joy he called "Northernness,"
a stern and ecstatic vision of things "cold, spacious, severe, pale,
and remote."

Of course, nature itself could also be a direct source of Joy for
the young Lewis. From earliest childhood Jack and Warren would
look out beyond bustling Belfast and gaze at the low line of the
Castlereagh Hills, cool and serene above the city of cinders. These
hills, on the seemingly unreachable horizon, called out to him, bid
him come, evoking that familiar longing and ache and pleasure.
Looking back, Lewis would note the effect those hills had on his
childhood imagination, saying that they created in him a longing
for unattainable horizons, making him, before he even started
school, "a votary of the Blue Flower."

"The blue flower" is a term from German romanticism used to
symbolize the longing for some unknown object. Even more reso-
nant in the original German, *"blaue Blume,"* the phrase was
coined by Novalis (1772-1801) to connote an intense yearning for
infinity. Lewis came to believe that this yearning, which he experienced long before he had a name for it, was not so much for infin-

ity as for the Infinite. As he so often did, Lewis took an idea that appealed to him and "Christianized" it, making his own search for that elusive Joy the focus of his own spiritual pilgrimage.

Even when he first experienced Joy as a child, Lewis recognized that the feeling was not mere nostalgia or love of nature. It was a desire, then, for what? Trying to answer that question became a kind of personal grail quest for Jack, a quest he would recount first in his highly autobiographical allegory, *The Pilgrim's Regress,* and again in his memoir, *Surprised by Joy.* Both books are organized around the search for Joy, trying and setting aside many false objects of "Sweet Desire," until one finally comes to rest in humble recognition of the true Object one has been seeking since childhood.

For Lewis, childhood came to an abrupt end when his mother, at the age of forty-six, was diagnosed with cancer and passed away within seven months. That was a harrowing time for the whole Lewis family, and for Warren and Jack the period of decline was no less traumatic than the death itself. For the boys, the bereavement began several months before the death, as their mother was withdrawn from them into the hands of doctors and nurses, while the house became a place of alien medicinal smells, late-night footsteps in the hallway and whispered conversations.

Besides losing his mother, Jack in a very real sense lost his father and his home as well. Even before the onset of Flora's illness, young Jack had described his father in a little daybook as a man with a "bad temper, very sensible, nice when not in a bad temper." In his teenage years Lewis would speculate that his father's moods were related to alcohol, and in his twenties he would frankly confess that, as a child, he had been afraid of his father.

As to Flora's death, Lewis felt that his father never fully recovered from the loss. Albert's grieving was apparently the sort that pushes others away rather than drawing them closer. He had always been a highly emotional man, and this great sorrow made him behave unpredictably, sometimes berating his sons for no good reason. Lewis would later observe that during these months Albert unfortunately lost his sons nearly as completely as he lost his wife. The anguished time of Flora's decline and death set a pattern of strained relations between Jack and his father that would persist for over two decades until 1929, when Albert fell into his own last illness.

At this point readers may be wondering why a study of Lewis's spiritual pilgrimage is dwelling so long on "emotional" factors, such as the loss of his mother in childhood and a prolonged estrangement from his father. After all, Lewis was the first to insist that one should embrace Christianity because it is *true*, not because it is therapeutic. In "Man or Rabbit?" (1946), for example, Lewis affirms that his faith is founded on reality, not on psychology: "Christianity is not a patent medicine. Christianity claims to give an account of *facts*—to tell you what the real universe is like. . . . If Christianity is untrue, then no honest man will want to believe it, however helpful it might be: if it is true, every honest man will want to believe it, even if it gives him no help at all."

Yet if Lewis maintained that one's sense of reality was not reducible to emotional needs, he was also aware that emotional imbalances might indeed distort one's sense of reality. In an essay on George MacDonald, Lewis concedes that Freud may be correct in assuming that "distortions in character and errors in thought result from a man's early conflicts with his father." But Lewis goes on to say that MacDonald's life reveals the opposite process, that his close relationship with his father was a tremendous source of strength for him and it taught him that Fatherhood lay at the very center of the cosmos. Thus, in what Lewis calls an "anti-Freudian predicament," MacDonald's theological insights about God the Father were clearly grounded in his childhood family experiences.

Of course, the relationship between psychology and theology is a vast and nebulous topic, one which goes far beyond any single study of Lewis or MacDonald. Freud's psychoanalytic theories have been widely questioned, and he seems to many scholars now less a social scientist than a sort of modernist mystic, one who sought to discover fundamental realities by looking inward rather than upward. Yet humans often do think and act with only a dim awareness of their own motives; if Freud had not existed, it might be necessary to invent him.

Paul Vitz has made an intriguing contribution to this discussion in his book *Faith of the Fatherless: The Psychology of Atheism*. Vitz argues that it was influential skeptics such as Feuerbach and Freud who first proposed to "explain" religious belief not as a question of truth but in terms of emotional needs. Christians, according to these theorists, are among the psychologically needy who project a benevolent, all-protecting Father into the heavens, far more powerful and caring than their flawed earthly fathers. But such ad hominem analysis, notes Vitz, is "a double-edged sword that can also, indeed easily, be used to explain their unbelief." Vitz asserts that "atheism of the strong or intense type is to a substantial degree generated by the peculiar psychological needs of its advocates," usually associated with defective father figures.

Not content with broad generalities, Vitz goes on to examine the lives of prominent skeptics, and he reveals that in case after case—Voltaire, David Hume, Friedrich Nietzsche, Bertrand Russell, Jean-Paul Sartre and many others—there is a missing or estranged father. Vitz includes quotations from the standard biographies demonstrating how often the most widely known skeptics have expressed resentment toward their fathers for abandoning them, dismissing religion as an institution for women and so on. By contrast, the most notable Christian leaders and thinkers (as Lewis observed of George MacDonald) have enjoyed unusually strong and loving bonds with their fathers and regarded them as major role models.

This is a precarious sort of analysis, and, as Vitz notes, it is the kind of sword which can cut in both directions. It seems rather glib for either believers or unbelievers to presume that one's own views are based on unflinching analysis while those who disagree are dominated by unconscious emotional conflicts. But it seems safe to assume that while one cannot "explain" someone's faith in terms of emotional needs and childhood experiences, one may well discover *obstacles* to faith that are rooted in childhood.

For C. S. Lewis, according to his own recollections, the key childhood experiences which formed the starting point for his spiritual journey were "the troubles" in Ireland, his encounters with Joy, his father's volatile temperament and the untimely loss of his beloved mother. As mentioned above, Lewis viewed this last bereavement as the end of his childhood: "With my mother's death all settled happiness, all that was tranquil and reliable, disappeared from my life. There was to be much fun, many pleasures, many stabs of Joy; but no more of the old security. It was sea and islands now; the great continent had sunk like Atlantis." This somber conclusion calls to mind a passage in the book of Hebrews: "People who speak thus make it clear that they are seeking a homeland. . . . They desire a better country, that is, a heavenly one" (Heb 11:14, 16 RSV). For nine-year-old Jack, the search for that better country was only beginning—and he would start by leaving his own homeland less than a month after the death of his mother.

TWO

THE ALIEN TERRITORY OF BOYHOOD

For C. S. Lewis the end of childhood was the beginning of boyhood. In Lewis's terminology boyhood is a regrettable state, which for him was characterized by intellectual languor, gregariousness instead of friendship, and a religious life that was at first oppressive and then irrelevant. During these years Lewis also experienced a cessation of Joy, pursuing instead more prosaic pleasures which lasted throughout his six years in English boarding schools.

Even before he left Belfast to board a ferry for England, the young Jack, not yet ten, seemed to sense a dreadful change in the air. Describing his first set of school clothes in *Surprised by Joy,* Lewis recalls wistfully the freedom and comfort of a child's playwear and then comments on the misery of his new uniform. He left home in new clothes which made him sweat and itch, boots that made his feet ache and a bowler hat that grasped his head like an iron band. Once he and Warren had crossed over to England, the signs looked no more promising. The countryside celebrated in poetry as "Green Hertfordshire" looked to a young Irish lad flat, flinty and featureless, while English accents sounded to his ears like some strange demonic chatter.

But worse yet was the destination that awaited him. Wynyard School in Watford, Surrey, turned out to be a semi-detached house of ugly yellow brick, with one classroom and one dormitory, the latter a low-ceilinged room with curtainless windows and one washbasin to be shared by all the boys. There was no library, no laboratory and no athletic field; the sickroom doubled as a lumber room, and the playground was just an open space covered more with gravel than grass. Writing about this wretched place years later, Warren Lewis said that the stench of the outdoor toilets was one of his strongest memories of the school, facilities which "even in 1905 any Sanitary Inspector would have unhesitatingly condemned."

C. S. Lewis's recollections of Wynyard were just as negative as his brother's. In *Surprised by Joy* Lewis calls the school Belsen, after the Nazi concentration camp. He was abjectly miserable there, for as bad as the school facility was, its master was even worse. Robert Capron, called "Oldie" by the boys, was an arbitrary and sadistic man, whose frequent rages were accompanied by canings and severe verbal abuse. Capron cared little for learning, treating history as an endless recitation of names and dates, and geography as a meaningless list of countries, cities, towns and rivers. As for mathematics, Warren Lewis recalled that he sat at his desk one whole term working out the same four sums on his slate, with no instruction or supervision. Capron also cared nothing for little boys; he seemed almost to relish his pupils' mistakes as a chance to inflict a caning. In one instance he behaved so brutally that a student's family brought a court action against him, which was settled out of court in favor of the plaintiff.

The conditions at the school—a lack of hot meals, of decent sanitation and of any concern for genuine learning—sound like something out of Dickens. Readers have wondered if Lewis did not exaggerate the privations and the brutality of life at Wynyard in *Surprised by Joy,* but his memories are confirmed by his brother's memoirs and by other unfortunates who attended the school at the same time as the Lewis brothers. In fact, the school closed down two years after Jack arrived there, and Oldie was later certified as insane. A few months before Jack's death in 1963, he wrote that, after half a century of effort, he had finally forgiven the man who had so scarred his earliest boyhood.

In *Surprised by Joy* Lewis explains that his father chose this odious school not by thinking too little about it, but by thinking too much. He compares his father to the man in Earle's "Skepticke in Religion" who "is alwayes too hard for himself," being simple-minded just when he thinks he is subtle. But the surviving family correspondence clearly shows that *both* parents were involved in the choice of Wynyard, and that their mother, Flora, took Warren there herself for the first time in 1905. So it was she, and not Albert, who had the opportunity to see the school facilities firsthand, a detail that illustrates the Lewis brothers' tendency to idealize their lost mother and to be too hard on their father. Children do not always do their parents justice, sometimes seeing them more in terms of what they are not than what they are. Lewis recognized this fault in himself in later years, but even so, this instance reminds us that his judgments of his father do not always give us a fully rounded picture.

It may be asked, if conditions at Wynyard were so intolerable, why didn't Warren and Jack complain to their parents? The answer is that they did, but apparently their parents dismissed this as homesickness and, in their father's words, the usual "friction be-

tween a master and his pupils." In February 1908, Warren wrote
home that Capron had told him even Mrs. Lewis considered her elder son a complete failure. Flora replied unequivocally that she
had never said or thought such a thing. She died the following
summer, and by the autumn, after Jack had joined Warren, both
brothers were writing their father about conditions at Wynyard.
The elder brother reported to his father that Capron derided both
boys for being Irish, that he accused Warren of stealing and called
him "an infernal hog." Jack wrote to add that he'd overheard Capron curse Warren out loud, pleading that they be withdrawn from
that "hole" before the term was up. Albert responded this time by
writing Capron, saying he was considering withdrawing his sons
from the school; Capron replied with an unctuous letter praising
"Jacko" in unmeasured terms and reporting that Warren was "quite
his old self again" and no longer presented any disciplinary prob-
lems. Apparently this was enough to smooth things over, for Warren finished out the year at Wynyard and Jack returned there again
the following year, 1909-1910.

In *Surprised by Joy* Lewis accepts part of the blame for his father's never understanding just how miserable the conditions were
at the school he called Belsen. He explains that no boy wants to
be considered "a coward and a crybaby," and that if he'd discussed
candidly what he'd been through at school, he would have had to
confess himself to have been for three months "a pale, quivering,
tear-stained, obsequious slave." Of the schoolboy's depiction of his
tormentor, Lewis observes, "He would rather represent his master
as a buffoon than an ogre."

As an adult, Lewis seems to have followed this same coping
strategy. In 1955, the year he published *Surprised by Joy,* portraying Capron as an ogre, he also published *The Magician's Nephew,*
portraying him as a buffoon. Lewis's imaginative transformation of

the brutal Capron into the comical Ketterley illustrates the process sometimes referred to as "shedding one's sicknesses in books."

Even in physical description, one is struck by the parallels: Uncle Andrew is described in *The Magician's Nephew* as "very tall and very thin," "with a sharp nose and extremely bright eyes"—these last also called "awful eyes" by Digory. He also has "a great mop of tousled grey hair," which is referred to a half dozen times in the course of the story. Later in the book we also learn that Uncle Andrew has turned sixty. In the Lewis family memoirs, Warren judges Capron to have been "about 60" when the Lewis brothers attended Wynyard, describing him as "above middle height" with "piercing eyes" which were nearly black, a small, deformed nose which appeared varnished and "plentiful grey hair." Capron was also remembered for his "Assyrian smile," suggesting not good will but guile—which reminds us of Uncle Andrew's malicious grin, variously described as a "cunning smile," a "cruel smile" and a "hateful smile."

Though Uncle Andrew is an insidious character, he is also one of Lewis's most successful comic creations. Despite the many parallels, Andrew is ultimately someone who evokes not dread or loathing but laughter. In this instance, Lewis's parody seems to be a kind of pardon. By turning an ogre into a buffoon, he was able to transform fear and anger into pity and forgiveness—using his imagination to purge his heart and to prepare his soul for the absolution he would finally achieve after half a century of trying.

Lewis considered his boyhood years to be unfortunate not only for what happened *to* him but also for what happened *within* him. He reports that there was a serious decline in his imaginative life during his boarding school days, adding that his childhood quest for Joy was all but forgotten. He attributes this partly to the trite school stories he read during that time, arguing that children's

reading is actually less escapist than the books they read a few
years later. After all, a nursery book like *Peter Rabbit* may engage
children's imaginations without their wanting to become rabbits,
but the school story about an awkward novice who becomes a star
varsity player is designed to feed a young person's actual fantasies
and ambitions.

This contrast between childhood and boyhood recurs throughout Lewis's account of his boarding school years. He recalls, for
example, that one of the few pleasures at Wynyard was conversing
with his fellow sufferers who, he says, still shared the broad curiosity of children, not the stiflingly narrow interests of schoolboys.

The most resounding critique of boyhood comes in a key passage in *Surprised by Joy* where Lewis sums up his boarding school
years. He depicts adolescence, the twilight of boyhood, as a kind
of renaissance, an awakening from the "dark ages." He argues that
the dreams of childhood and those of early adulthood have much
in common, but that in between there stretches an "alien territory
in which everything (ourselves included) has been greedy, cruel,
noisy, and prosaic, in which the imagination has slept." Lewis concludes that his own childhood was at unity with the rest of his life,
his boyhood a long, unprofitable interruption.

Lewis's early boyhood *was* at unity with the rest of his life in
one respect: religious questions occupied his thoughts a great deal
during his time at Wynyard. Part of the regimen there was manda-
tory church attendance twice every Sunday at a nearby church
with high Anglican services. A diary entry from 1909 makes it clear
that young Jack's early impressions were extremely negative: "We
are obliged to go to St. John's, a church which wanted to be Roman Catholic but was afraid to say so. A kind of church abhorred
by all respectful Irish Protestants. In this abominable place of Rom-
ish hypocrites and English liars, the people cross themselves, bow

to the Lord's Table (which they have the vanity to call an altar) and pray to the Virgin."

This passage has a unique place in the Lewis archive, for it is the only anti-Catholic diatribe one finds anywhere in his writings, either published or unpublished. Lewis recalled in *Surprised by Joy* that his first reaction to the church was negative—though he prudently chose not to quote this passage in his memoir. He explained the initial hostility he felt as that of a northern Irish lad still feeling very much the stranger in a strange land: "Was I not an Ulster Protestant, and were not these unfamiliar rituals an essential part of the hated English atmosphere?"

As Lewis himself recognized, his initial reaction to St. John's reflected not only where he was but also where he had been. In later years Lewis would use the term "Puritanism" to describe the self-righteous indignation and sectarian bigotry that appear in the diary entry he wrote as a boy. In his scholarly books he explained that the actual Puritans of history were the radicals and revolutionaries of their era, not conservatives or fundamentalists, and that what they opposed was "bishops not beer." But he also noted that the sixteenth-century Puritans were typified by "moral severity" and that their writings were full of denunciation and censoriousness.

For Lewis the severity of the historic Puritans was an outgrowth of their moral earnestness, their desire to close the gap between "the life of 'religion' and the life of the world." But he called those who surrounded him in his youth "apostate Puritans," people for whom spiritual vigor had been replaced by legalistic rigor. In a letter to his childhood friend Arthur Greeves, Lewis refers to the dominant creed of Ulster as "Puritanism," defining it as the "*memory* of Christianity." This is the kind of religion, notes Lewis, in which the true marks of faith—"peace, love, wisdom, and humility"—have been replaced by sectarian narrowness and a quickness to judge others.

Lewis offers another glimpse of contemporary Puritanism in *The Pilgrim's Regress* (1933), an allegorical tale with strong autobiographical overtones. This was the first book Lewis wrote after returning to Christianity in his early thirties, and he produced it in a white heat of creativity and intellectual zeal, writing out the whole book longhand in two weeks during a stay in Belfast with his old friend Arthur. (The Greeves family lived just down the road from the Lewises, and the two boys had known each other since childhood. Their true friendship, though, began when the fifteen-year-old Jack discovered that Arthur, three years older, shared his passion for "Northernness" and many of his other literary interests. The two friends exchanged letters and visits for nearly half a century, until Lewis's death in 1963.)

The Pilgrim's Regress, which is dedicated to Greeves, begins with these simple words: "I dreamed of a boy who was born in the land of Puritania and his name was John." In the first chapter, called "The Rules," John is taken to visit a Steward for instruction about "the Landlord," their concept of God. Before he can enter into the presence of the imposing Steward, John is forced to put on new clothes, which "caught him under the chin and were tight under the arms" and "made him itch all over"—rather like the clothes young Jack had to wear the day he was first sent away from home.

The Steward seems approachable enough at first, but then he dons a ceremonial beard, affects a peculiar sing-song voice and shows John a big card full of the Landlord's rules. John is overwhelmed by the sheer number of rules, and also because so many rules forbid things he's never heard of or else they forbid everyday activities he thought were a normal part of living. The Steward warns sternly that if John breaks any of the rules and displeases the Landlord, he will be shut up "for ever and ever in a black hole full of snakes and scorpions as large as lobsters." When John quails and asks how to avoid this dreadful place, the Steward launches into an abstruse explanation far above John's comprehension, concluding that "the Landlord is extraordinarily kind and good to his tenants, and would certainly torture most of them to death the moment he had the slightest pretext." While John's head is still spinning from all this, the Steward takes off the mask, hands John the card and then whispers in the boy's ear that he needn't really concern himself about all this.

Of course, in the older Lewis's understanding, this is the kind of teaching one needs to escape from in order to come to true faith. The Steward does not offer salvation by grace through faith, but rather a comprehensive legalistic code, so detailed and arbitrary that it can only lead to moral exhaustion or hypocrisy. But Jack's view of God in his early boyhood did not differ greatly from that of his alter ego, John. (Of course, it goes without saying that the nickname Jack usually stands for John, not Clive.)

In *Surprised by Joy* Lewis recalls that he first came to "serious belief" during his Wynyard years, but that serious faith was also a joyless faith. After his negative first response to services at St. John's, he found that he was gradually being influenced by hearing the doctrines of the Christian faith expounded by people who clearly believed in them and considered them vital. Unfortunately, his newfound beliefs did not provide him assurance or comfort but rather self-condemnation. As Lewis explains it, he fell into an internalized legalism, by which his private prayers never seemed good enough, because he always harbored doubts about whether he was praying with sufficient earnestness. Too often, he felt, his lips were saying the right things but his mind and heart were not in the words. Of course, one can will what to do, but one cannot will what to feel, and so he became oppressed by the "ludicrous burden of false duties in prayer."

And so the lonely little boy imprisoned himself in a religion of guilt, not grace. Lewis vividly recalls lying awake fearing for his soul on "certain blazing moonlit nights in that curtainless dormitory" at Wynyard. The memory of the "ghastly beauty of the full moon" occurs three more times in *Surprised by Joy;* the memory was obviously a vivid one, even forty years later. To the young boy who had lost his mother and been sent away from his father into the hands of a brutal schoolmaster, that oppressive moon must have seemed almost like the eye of an angry god, glaring down in disapproval.

It is interesting to note that in the fiction Lewis would later write, many of the most spiritually charged moments, both positive and negative, occur by the light of a blazing full moon. In *Out of the Silent Planet,* Ransom's adventures begin when he is drugged and carried into a rocket ship headed for Mars. Awakening in the middle of the journey, he sees a "portentous moon" out the window, impossibly large and blindingly white. He feels he is poised on an emotional watershed between "delirious terror" and "an ecstasy of joy" before he eventually adjusts his perspective and realizes that the "megalomaniac disk" out the window is actually the planet earth as seen from space. In *That Hideous Strength* "the Moon in all her wildness" appears one cold, cloudless night, suggesting not sentimental love songs, but rather "the huntress, the untameable virgin, the spear-head of madness." For Mark Studdock, in the midst of his spiritual descent, the sight is unnerving; but for his wife Jane, whose spiritual healing has begun, it is an exhilarating vision.

For the young Lewis, such a moon, and such a faith, were not exhilarating but oppressive, and it seems the "serious belief" of his

Wynyard days did not long outlast his stay there. After leaving Wynyard, Lewis spent a brief stint at Campbell College, only a mile from his father's house in Belfast. Though he did not stay at Campbell long enough to develop vivid impressions, his time there reinforced his sense of rootlessness. As a nonresident student, he felt that he was always "moving on" or "hanging about"—in corridors, empty classrooms, even the lavatory—feeling rather like a homeless person living in a large railway station.

Lewis left Campbell because of ill health, and the following term, at the age of twelve, he went to Cherbourg House in Worcestershire, a preparatory school for Malvern College. (In America we would think of Cherbourg as a private middle school and Malvern not as a college but as a prep school.) Jack was much happier at Cherbourg. One can almost measure Lewis's emotional response to the schools he attended by the degree to which they simulated a home environment. His relative contentment at Cherbourg House is clearly linked to the matron there, who acted as a surrogate mother for the boys. Lewis describes her with the same unabashed affection he had expressed in his earlier depiction of his childhood nurse. He concludes his portrait of the matron at Cherbourg House with a revelatory summation: "We all loved her; I, the orphan, especially."

Ironically, the matron at Cherbourg who served for a time as a surrogate mother for Lewis was also the means by which he set aside his childhood faith. Though selfless and good-natured, she was, according to Lewis, spiritually immature, uncritically drawn to occultism and to esoteric philosophies. Her speculations created in her young pupil a feeling that Christianity was only one way of looking at spiritual realities—and not necessarily the most compelling one. Added to this came a growing knowledge of other religions and a sense that if other religions were mere expressions of their time and culture, then might not Christianity be merely an expression of its culture?

In many a young person on the threshold of puberty, such a faith crisis might also become an emotional crisis. But Lewis recalls that he became an unbeliever with a great sense of relief, not regret. To those skeptics who would dismiss religious belief as mere wish fulfillment, Lewis answers that losing one's faith can be as great a consolation as finding it. He reports that the dread of those wakeful nights under a glaring moon at Wynyard faded away once he passed from "the tyrannous noon of revelation" into "the cool evening" of skeptical reason, a state of mind in which "there was nothing to be obeyed, and nothing to be believed except what was either comforting or exciting."

In *The Pilgrim's Regress* Lewis shows even more vividly how liberating it can be to lose one's faith. Soon after his unsettling visit with the Steward, the boy John, struggling under the burden of all the rules he has broken, meets Mr. Enlightenment. After explaining that he was raised in Puritania, John finds his heart lifted up when Enlightenment tells him what a good place that is to leave. Though he is offered the flimsiest imaginable arguments against Christianity, John is only too glad to bow to Mr. Enlightenment's authority, and he becomes ecstatic over his newfound unbelief. "There is no Landlord," he exclaims, feeling so relieved he could almost take wing. Suddenly it seems that all of nature is glad, the frost gleaming like silver and the sky like blue glass. He sees a friendly robin hopping in a nearby bush and hears a cock crowing from somewhere out of sight. "There is no Landlord." John repeats gleefully, chuckling at the thought of the "old card of rules hung over his bed in the bedroom, so low and dark, in his father's house." Almost dazed with exhilaration, he cries out yet again, "There is no Landlord. There is no black hole." Clearly a great burden has rolled away—not a burden of sin but rather one of fear and self-accusation.

Besides losing his faith at Cherbourg, Lewis also felt that he lost his innocence there, as he succumbed to erotic fantasies. Having discovered sexual pleasure, the young Lewis wondered for a time if the elusive Joy he had been seeking as a child was really only sublimated lust. Before long, however, he concluded that there was nothing elusive about sexual longing and that its object was not at all remote or mysterious. Lewis felt that his own experience revealed to him a marked contrast between sexual desire and Sweet Desire, concluding, "You might as well offer a mutton chop to a man who's dying of thirst as offer sexual pleasure to the desire I am speaking of." If anything, according to Lewis, a Freudian approach put the case backwards: "Joy is not a substitute for sex; sex is very often a substitute for Joy."

While Jack discovered skepticism and sensuality at Cherbourg, he also learned about worldliness there. The matron was assisted by a worldly young instructor, called Pogo in *Surprised by Joy,* the seeming embodiment of adolescent sophistication whom the young Lewis sought eagerly to emulate. As he later explains, Lewis acquired from Pogo "the desire for glitter, swagger, distinction, the desire to be in the know." In his remaining years of boarding school young Jack made every effort to turn himself into "a fop, a cad, and a snob."

In later years Lewis would consistently associate flashiness, false sophistication, a pose of world-weary wisdom with the later years of his boyhood. In his essay "Shelley, Dryden, and Mr. Eliot" (1939), Lewis explained that some people, especially boys, like to call themselves "disillusioned, because the very form of the word suggests that they have had the illusions and emerged from them." He argues, however, that those who call themselves disenchanted are really unenchanted, imposters who have "never risen so high as to be in danger of the generous illusions they claim to have escaped from." He concludes that those who pose as "sages who have passed through the half-truths of humanitarian benevolence, aristocratic honour, or romantic passion" are more likely to be "clods who have never yet advanced so far."

But if the pose of "disillusionment" can be itself a kind of illusion, young Jack's disillusionment with the religion of his Wynyard years seems to have been a necessary forward step. In some cases it may be necessary to lose one's faith in order to save it.

THREE

MERE ATHEISM IN
EARLY ADOLESCENCE

W hen Lewis in later years called materialism "a philosophy
for boys," he was speaking dismissively, but also autobiographi-
cally: Materialism was the philosophy that dominated his boyhood
after the two years at Wynyard. Indeed, one of his friends from his
prep school days described him as a "riotously amusing atheist."
The same friend said he was "staggered" years later when he
learned that the C. S. Lewis who wrote *The Screwtape Letters* was
the same "foul mouthed" Jack Lewis he had known as a teenager.

Having lost his faith while at Cherbourg House, Jack found his
unbelief strengthened in succeeding years from several directions.
The first was that perennial dilemma which confronts anyone who
professes a philosophy of hope: the problem of evil. For Christians
the specific question is, how could a God who is all-good and all-
powerful create and rule a world in which there is so much suffering and injustice? As if this issue in itself was not worthy of somber
contemplation, Jack's adolescent atheism was further reinforced by

his reading in the natural and social sciences. From the former he gained a sense that life on earth is just a random occurrence in a vast, empty universe, that all of human history is no more than a teardrop in the vast ocean of eternity. From the latter he concluded that all the world's religions, including Christianity, could be best explained not as claims to truth, but as expressions of psychological needs and cultural values.

Lewis's philosophical pessimism remained fairly constant through these years, even as his sense of personal contentment varied widely with changing circumstances. Moving from Cherbourg House, with its motherly matron and worldly assistant schoolmaster, to prep school, he again became intensely unhappy. The regimentation and the required games there were a trial for Jack. Even more, he despised the social hierarchy in which the in-group, or "Bloods"—most often athletes—were accorded privilege and prestige, and before whom the others were supposed to grovel.

Though Lewis certainly never aspired to be a "Blood" during his time at Malvern, he admits to becoming something of a prig. In his first letter to Arthur Greeves from Malvern, for example, Lewis described his fellow pupils as "coarse, brainless English schoolboys" whose thoughts seldom rose above meals and games and homework. Of course, it is not surprising that a young man of such highly developed literary sensibilities should feel out of place among his stolid schoolmates.

While at Malvern, Jack wrote a play called *Loki Bound,* a retelling of Norse myth which pitted the "sad wisdom" of Loki against the "brutal orthodoxy" of Odin. In later years Lewis recognized that the rebellious Loki represented himself and the repressive regime of Odin symbolized the "Bloods" at Malvern. He also commented later on the paradoxical pessimism of this early work, saying that in his adolescence he did not believe there was a God, yet he resented God for not existing. Further still, he resented this God who was or wasn't there for creating such a flawed world.

At first, Jack's situation at Malvern made him feel that he stood alone against the world. But eventually he found a few friends who shared his literary tastes, and he developed a sense of "we few, we band of brothers," so that the world of the Bloods became only one world, a world of "Games and Gallantry" that he need not submit to. As he grew older, Lewis became accustomed to this stance and even began to revel in it. England's perilous stand in 1940 before a seemingly invincible Germany felt familiar to him, and he later relished his role as torchbearer for "we few" against the armies of progressivism, collectivism and modernism in general.

At the age of fifteen, however, Lewis was not ready to take on the world. He wrote repeatedly to his father asking to be removed from Malvern, eventually threatening to shoot himself unless his father allowed him to withdraw. Accordingly, Albert Lewis sent him to live with a private tutor named William Kirkpatrick, who ran a small "cramming school" in Great Bookham, Surrey. "Kirk," or the "Great Knock" (as he was dubbed by the Lewis family), had been the schoolmaster at Lurgan College near Belfast, which Albert had attended and where he had accumulated a great many fond, if sentimental, memories.

Kirkpatrick turned out to be utterly unlike the mawkish reminiscences Albert had shared with his sons. He was a forthright and skeptical man, a pugnacious atheist of the old-fashioned Thomas Huxley variety. Lewis says he "came near to being a purely logical entity," who considered even the most casual remark as a "summons to disputation." Many a teenager would have quavered under such a teacher, but the young Lewis enjoyed the intellectual challenge and the rigorous standards of logical precision. He thrived under this style of tutoring as "red beef and strong beer." (In Lewis's later fiction, Kirkpatrick would reappear in the guise of MacPhee, the humorless, freethinking Ulsterman in *That Hideous Strength*.)

The two and a half years Jack spent at Great Bookham were some of the most personally settled of his young life, but they were also a time for some of his bleakest philosophical reflections. Kirkpatrick was an outspoken skeptic who had Lewis reading Arthur Schopenhauer's withering critiques of religion as well as James Frazier's *The Golden Bough*. From Schopenhauer's books Jack gained a sense that the universe was a random cosmic event, and that all religions were futile attempts by fearful humans to control the great forces of nature before which they felt so powerless. From *The Golden Bough*, a comprehensive work on comparative religions and mythology published in twelve volumes (1890-1915), Lewis came to feel that religion was simply an expression of culture, that all peoples had their own myths and legends, just as they had their own customs, and that no one system of beliefs, such as Christianity, was any more "true" than any other. Ironically, Frazier's uneven and methodologically flawed work has been largely set aside by later generations of anthropologists and is now remembered mainly for its literary influence on authors such as T. S. Eliot and James Joyce. But Lewis later wrote that Kirkpatrick "doted on *The Golden Bough*," a book which became a cornerstone of the young Lewis's atheism.

During those years Lewis was also reading scientific popularizers like H. G. Wells and Robert Ball who emphasized the "vastness and cold of space, the littleness of Man," making him feel that humans on their little spinning speck of dust were of very little account in a huge and empty cosmos. Lewis says he had formulated his own "Argument from Undesign" long before he encountered a quotation from Lucretius which summed it up for him:

> Had God designed the world, it would not be
> A world so frail and faulty as we see.

Anyone who doubts that Lewis felt the force of atheism in his youth need only consult the opening paragraphs of *The Problem of Pain* (1940), where he presents the case for nihilism about as cogently as it can be made. There he explains that when he was an atheist not that many years before, he would have explained his unbelief by pointing to the cosmos, mostly dark, empty and cold, and to our own world, which hung blindly in space for millions of years before any life appeared on its surface. Then he would add that life itself is dominated by one species preying on another, that even the best of lives end in death and that the "highest" life form, humans, have become conscious of all this, an awareness leading only to pain and despair. Given these facts, Lewis sums up his earlier case for unbelief:

> All stories will come to nothing: all life will turn out in the end to have been a transitory and senseless contortion upon the idiotic face of infinite matter. If you ask me to believe that this is the work of a benevolent and omnipotent spirit, I reply that all the evidence points in the opposite direction. Either there is no spirit behind the universe, or else a spirit indifferent to good and evil, or else an evil spirit.

Not surprisingly, in Lewis's books of Christian apologetics he never tried to argue for the existence of a benevolent Creator based on what we can deduce from creation. Yet even as a young man Jack came to recognize that if all positive philosophies have the problem of evil to grapple with, negative philosophies have an opposite dilemma, a problem of good. That is, if the universe is essentially meaningless and humankind bound for nothing more than eventual extinction, then where do our ideals of what life *ought* to be like come from?

In his essay "De Futilitate" (1940), Lewis confesses that in his youth he wrote reams of poetry amplifying on a line he found in A. E. Housman about "whatever brute and blackguard made the world." But eventually he realized there was a catch in his stance of heroic pessimism: "If a Brute and Blackguard made the world, then he also made our minds. If he made our minds, he also made that very standard whereby we judge him to be a Brute and Blackguard. And how can we trust a standard which comes from such a brutal and blackguardly source?" In other words, if you reject God because there is so much evil in the universe, you are obliged to explain from whence you obtained your standard for discerning good and evil.

In the same essay Lewis goes on to argue that those who deny any ultimate source for human rationality have the same kind of problem as those who deny any foundation for human morality. That is, how are their own declarations to be judged? One may try to argue that human reason has no logical relation to reality, that it is merely an evolutionary survival mechanism. But such radical skepticism about human thought is self-refuting. If human thought is dismissed as merely the brain activity of one particular species, why should that thought itself be believed? How does this very definition itself correlate to the reality outside human heads? Lewis sums up the paradox aptly: "Is the thought that no thoughts are true, itself true? If we answer Yes, we contradict ourselves. For if all thoughts are untrue, then this thought is untrue. There is therefore no question of total skepticism about human thought."

Eventually the young Lewis came to recognize that his brand

of atheism was riddled with such contradictions. As for the forbidding picture of the "vastness and cold of space, the littleness of Man" which Jack had encountered in his reading of H. G. Wells and others, he would later see this as an imaginative problem, not an intellectual one. It is commonly thought that the medieval mind pictured a cozy little universe with our world at its center, the apple of God's eye, and that it took modern science to reveal the cosmos to be an unimaginably vast expanse. But Lewis points out in several of his books that, as far back as Ptolemy, it was recognized that the earth was an infinitesimal point in relation to the fixed stars, one ancient authority calculating the distance to be 117 million miles.

What was different about the medieval worldview was its way of conceptualizing space, so that those under a starry sky felt they were looking *up,* not *out,* as if "being conducted through an immense cathedral, not like one lost in a shoreless sea." Lewis does not feel that the immensity of the universe as revealed by modern science has as much spiritual significance as some have supposed, since ten million miles or ten billion are much the same to our finite minds; they can be conceived, but not really imagined. And physical size in itself is no measure of spiritual value, lest a tree be considered more important than a human.

Lewis ultimately suggests that the unimaginable expanse of the physical universe should not create despair over the minuteness of our world, the brevity of our lives or the futility of our hopes. Rather it may be contemplated as the garment of God, a physical metaphor for his infinite nature. Instead of being terrified, like Pascal, with "the eternal silence of infinite spaces," Lewis invites his readers to reenvision space—and spatiality. After opening his book *The Problem of Pain* on the note of materialistic despair that he remembered from his youth, Lewis concludes that work by reinterpreting the same vast cosmos as a mystical symbol of its Creator:

> The size and emptiness of the universe which frightened us at the
> outset of this book, should awe us still, for though it may be no
> more than a subjective by-product of our three-dimensional imagin-
> ing, yet they symbolise great truth. As our Earth is to all the stars, so
> doubtless are we men and our concerns to all creation; as all the
> stars are to space itself, so are all we creatures, all thrones and pow-
> ers and the mightiest of the created gods, to the abyss of the self-ex-
> isting Being, who is to us Father and Redeemer and indwelling
> Comforter, but of whom no man or angel can say nor conceive
> what He is in and for Himself, or what is the work that he "maketh
> from beginning to the end." For they are all derived and unsubstan-
> tial things. Their vision fails them and they cover their eyes from the
> intolerable light of utter actuality, which was and is and shall be,
> which never could have been otherwise, which has no opposite.

In addition to these philosophical and scientific issues, Lewis's
skepticism during his Great Bookham years was fueled by his tute-
lage under Kirkpatrick in what were then the fledgling social sciences. "The Great Knock" seems to have viewed all religion with a
certain benign sociological detachment—all, that is, except for
Christianity. When Jack's father mentioned in a letter that one of
the universities was considering adding a chair in medieval philosophy, Kirkpatrick could hardly contain his indignation. He replied
irritably that in an era when the emerging social sciences could increasingly explain the origins of humans, as well as their religion,
it was simply absurd to bind young minds in "the fetters of an ig-
norant past." He could see no reason why young people should
study outdated philosophies from "an age of superstition" when
they ought to be focusing on "truth, so far as it can be known."

Apart from revealing Kirkpatrick's virulent skepticism, this letter
makes one wonder how Albert responded to this sort of diatribe. It

seems odd that a father would feel comfortable leaving his son's education to a man capable of such vehement outbursts against the faith Albert heard preached from his family pew at St. Mark's in Belfast every Sunday.

What Albert thought about all this is not known, but it is clear that Jack learned his lessons well. When Arthur Greeves, still affirming the tenets of his conservative Protestant parents, wrote to Jack in the autumn of 1916 asking about his beliefs, Lewis responded at length:

> You ask me my religious views: you know, I think, that I believe in no religion. There is absolutely no proof for any of them, and from a philosophical standpoint Christianity is not even the best. All religions, that is, all mythologies to give them their proper name, are merely man's own invention—Christ as much as Loki.

Lewis goes on to explain that early humans were surrounded by fearful and unfathomable powers of nature—punishing storms, wasting diseases, dangerous beasts. People just assumed there must be hostile spirits behind the terrible face of nature. Attempts to appease these spirits by offering songs or sacrifices eventually evolved into more formalized religions. He adds that human heroes such as Hercules, Odin or "a Hebrew philosopher Yeshua (whose name we have corrupted into Jesus)" came to be regarded as gods after their time on earth. In the latter case the cult that developed around Yeshua came to be associated with the tradition of "ancient Hebrew Yahweh worship" and so a new religion was born. The young Lewis concludes that Christianity is just "one mythology among many, but the one that we happen to have been brought up in."

This is about an equal mix of Schopenhauer and Frazier, seasoned with Kirkpatrick's peppery rhetoric. When Greeves challenged some of this analysis, Lewis responded again at length, this time in a more petulant tone. After dismissing the supernatural "tomfoolery" which had attached itself to the historical Jesus, Jack offers less an intellectual critique than an emotional response to Christian belief, as he then understood it. He says that he doesn't feel the need to believe in a "happy life hereafter," explaining sarcastically, "I am quite content to live without believing in a bogey who is prepared to torture me forever and ever if I should fail in coming to an almost impossible ideal." He concludes that he finds more comfort in unbelief than in belief, because it would be horrible for him to feel that if life got so bad he wanted to end it, he "daren't escape for fear of a spirit more cruel and barbarous than any man."

In *Surprised by Joy,* written nearly forty years later, Lewis looked back on his early exchanges with Greeves and seemed bothered more by the attitude than the analysis. He felt he had "exulted with youthful and vulgar pride" in what he considered his enlightened state, enjoying the thrust and parry of debate without realizing how simplistic and crude his arguments were. He comments dryly that at that age he was at the stage "in which a boy thinks it extremely telling to call God *Jahveh* and Jesus *Yeshua.*" Despite that later verdict, many readers will find in the young Lewis's letters an articulate and provocative critique of religion, coming as it does from the pen of a seventeen-year-old.

But perhaps the lad protests too much. Throughout his life, Lewis prized civility in debate, and the passages quoted above are among the most ill-tempered one finds anywhere in his writings, public or private. One cannot help but wonder if Arthur's probing questions acted as troubling reminders to the young Lewis of the deep-seated divisions he felt in his own nature, especially the split between the seeker and the debunker.

Lewis eventually developed a hearty skepticism for psychological or sociological "explanations" of religion such as those he fired off to Greeves during his Great Bookham years. Refuting, or rather reframing, Frazier would later be a major intellectual breakthrough for him, one which will be discussed in detail in chapter eight. But apart from the substance, it may be useful to note the *emotional tone* of Lewis's skepticism during this period of his life. Sometimes in his letters to Greeves he seems to go out of his way to make jibes about Christianity, even knowing how earnest Greeves and his family were about their faith. He complains that the weather in England has been as hot "as our future home down below" and jokes about how uncomfortable it must be for those four and twenty elders in the book of Revelation to bow down on a sea of glass. In another letter he takes up a phrase he has found in Maeterlinck, "the luminous ignorance of youth," and whimsically declares that it applies to both of them.

At that point in his life, Lewis seemed to equate the "luminous ignorance of youth" with Arthur's clinging to his childhood religion and with his own past search for Joy. He later explained that, after imbibing the "new Psychology," he began to dismiss his unattainable hills, his paradisal gardens and other images of Desire as mere wish-fulfillment fantasies: "With the confidence of a boy I decided I had done with all that. No more Avalon, no more Hesperides. I had (this is very precisely the opposite of the truth) 'seen through' them. And I was never going to be taken in again."

In those references to "seeing through" and not being "taken in," we again encounter specialized terms in Lewis's vocabulary. Both phrases refer to an attitude of false sophistication, a sense that one's penetrating scrutiny has stripped away the veil, revealed the true nature of what someone has been trying to fob off as a moral ideal, a spiritual insight or a deeper reality not visible to the senses.

In both Lewis's fiction and nonfiction, one finds the same spiritual obtuseness associated with those who claim they can *see through,* can avoid being *taken in.* In *Out of the Silent Planet,* when that dastardly duo, Weston and Devine, are brought to the island of Meldilorn to answer for their crimes, they hear a commanding voice in front of them but see nothing. Devine is astonished that the primitive inhabitants of that world (Mars) have somehow rigged up a loudspeaker, but Weston explains that it is some sort of ventriloquism performed by the local witch doctor, adding that the trick is to locate him and face him down to let him know you've "seen through him." What they do not realize is that they are in the presence of Oyarsa, the angelic sovereign of the planet. Similarly, in *The Last Battle* when the great lion Aslan tries to speak to the selfish dwarves to tell them they have entered the magnificent New Narnia, they continue to believe they are trapped in a dark stable, dismissing his growl as "a machine of some kind" and reassuring themselves, "They won't take *us* in again."

In his nonfiction Lewis offers a more systematic critique of the pose of "seeing through" or not being "taken in." In his essay "Meditation in a Toolshed" (1945), for example, Lewis begins by recounting an experience in which he was standing in a dark toolshed with only a beam of light coming in through a crack in the door. When he looked at the sunbeam, he saw nothing but specks of dust with darkness behind them. But when he moved so that the sunbeam fell across his eyes, he no longer saw the toolshed, or the sunbeam, but rather he could see outside—grass and trees and sky, even the sun ninety million miles away. He concludes, "Looking along the beam, and looking at the beam are very different experiences."

Lewis develops this thought by offering a series of contrasts between looking at and looking along: the way it feels to be in love versus the way a biologist would describe hormonal activity; the actual process of thinking versus brain function as a neuropsychologist might observe it. Then he asks, which is the truer picture: looking *at* or looking *along?* Someone standing beside him in the toolshed might discount his description of the world outside because all the observer could see from that vantage point was the sunbeam. As Lewis concludes, "In other words, you can stand outside one experience only by stepping inside another." You can't "see through" the experience of someone looking along a sunbeam, because you haven't aligned yourself with the sunbeam and are only looking *at* it.

In his essay "Bulverism" (1944), Lewis offered a more specific critique of Freudians and Marxists who felt they had "seen through" Christianity. He notes that the former reduce human thought and action to "bundles of complexes" and the latter to "economic interests," both dismissing Christian arguments for belief as "ideologically tainted." But how do they explain their own access to real causes without accounting for their own emotional conflicts or economic interests? How are the critics themselves immune from neurotic tendencies or class loyalties? It seems that all schools of thought rest on foundational axioms which must be assumed and not proven. Apparently, it is not merely Christians who embrace St. Augustine's formula, *Credo ut intelligam:* "I believe in order to understand."

To claim that you can simply see things for what they are without considering your own needs and interests ("what sort of person you are and where you are standing") suggests a vain combination of ignorance and arrogance. In *The Abolition of Man* (1947), Lewis points out why this sort of intellectual reductionism is ultimately self-defeating:

But you cannot go on "explaining away" for ever: you will find that you have explained explanation itself away. You cannot go on "seeing through" things for ever. The whole point of seeing through something is to see something through it. It is good that the window should be transparent, because the street or garden beyond it is opaque. How if you saw through the garden too? It is no use trying to "see through" first principles. If you see through everything, then everything is transparent. But a wholly transparent world is an invisible world. To "see through" all things is the same as not to see.

For Lewis radical skepticism was ultimately not at all visionary, but rather a form of spiritual blindness. He called materialism "a philosophy for boys" because, in the form he had known, it could not account for its own premises and because it too often promoted a kind of glib intellectual cynicism.

During his time with Kirkpatrick, Jack's need to reconcile his intellect with his imagination became more and more intertwined with the problem of developing a worldview that would satisfy both sides of his divided personality. Throughout these years his imagination, especially his glimpses of Joy, seemed to suggest some hidden glory at the center of things, while his intellect pointed in exactly the opposite direction. As will be seen in the next chapter, the Great Bookham years reveal a curious paradox in this stage of Jack's development: it seems the haughtier he became in intellect, the humbler he became in imagination.

FOUR

THE DUNGEON
OF A DIVIDED SOUL

After describing his early experiences of Joy and his loss of faith, Lewis would later describe his midteens as a time when the two hemispheres of his mind, intellect and imagination, were sharply divided. Part of his nature regaled in "a many-islanded sea of poetry and myth," while another side was dominated by "a glib and shallow rationalism." During that time Lewis said he lived daily with a nearly unendurable paradox: "Nearly all that I loved I believed to be imaginary; nearly all that I believed to be real I thought grim and meaningless."

Lewis's letters to Greeves during those years certainly bear out this retrospective judgment. Juxtaposed to rather bleak and polemical passages like those quoted in the previous chapter, one finds frequent and enthusiastic references to Lewis's "light reading." Apart from his study of Greek and Roman classics in the original languages, he was in his teens devouring texts for his own pleasure that many graduate students nowadays find difficult: Malory's

Morte d'Arthur, Sidney's *Arcadia,* Spenser's *Faerie Queene,* Milton's *Paradise Lost* and Bunyan's *Pilgrim's Progress.* He also took great pleasure in nineteenth-century fantasy classics such as William Morris's *The Well at the World's End,* as well as Matthew Arnold's poems on legend and myth such as "Balder Dead" and "Tristram and Isolt."

At the age of seventeen Lewis reached an early milestone in his spiritual journey, the discovery of George MacDonald's *Phantastes.* When he first read the story in the spring of 1916, Lewis wrote enthusiastically to Greeves that he'd had a "great literary experience" that week, and the book became one of his lifelong favorites. Over a decade later, Lewis wrote to Greeves that nothing gave him a sense of "spiritual healing, of being washed" as much as reading George MacDonald.

Phantastes (1858) is an episodic, dreamlike book, rich with spiritual overtones. It tells the story of a young man named Anodos, literally "one who has lost his way," whose mother died when he was a child. Reading a fairy tale one night, Anodos sighs that he wishes he could go to the world of fairy-country, and the next day he is indeed led into an enchanted wood. He meets a beautiful woman, the spirit of a beech-tree, who advises him about the dangers of her world and leaves him with a kiss, whose "cool faithfulness revives [his] heart wonderfully." He finds that he has come into a fuller harmony with the world of nature, understanding the conversation of the trees and animals and discovering within himself a "capacity for simple happiness" that he had never felt before.

Anodos soon encounters another beautiful young woman, this one pale and cold like marble (rather like the White Witch of Narnia), who tries to lure him to his destruction. He undergoes a series of adventures, including an encounter with an evil Ash tree and a sense of being followed by some shadow-creature of himself. Wearied almost to the point of despair, he plunges into a sparkling ocean on a starlit night and experiences a profound renewal of spirit:

> A blessing, like the kiss of a mother, seemed to alight on my soul; a calm, deeper than that which accompanies a hope deferred, bathed my spirit. . . . I felt as if once more the great arms of the beech-tree were around me, soothing me after the miseries I had passed through, and telling me, like a sick little child, that I should be better tomorrow. The waters of themselves lifted me, as with loving arms, to the surface.

After his swim, Anodos falls into a deep sleep and has "dreams of unspeakable joy—of restored friendships; of revived embraces; of love which said it had never died; of faces that had vanished long ago, yet said with smiling lips that they knew nothing of the grave; of pardons implored, and granted with such bursting floods of love."

At the end of the tale Anodos loses his life battling a giant wolf and discovers that even death itself is not dangerous:

> I was dead, and right content. I lay in my coffin with my hands folded in peace. . . . I felt as if a cool hand had been laid upon my heart and had stilled it. My soul was like a summer evening, after a heavy fall of rain, when the drops are yet glistening on the trees in the last rays of the down-going sun. The hot fever of life had gone by, and I breathed the clear mountain air of the land of Death. I had never dreamed of such blessedness.

After his death in fairy-country, Anodos returns to his own world, feeling that he has indeed found his way, that he has acquired "a power of calm endurance" that he had hitherto not known. The story ends on a note of resolution and hope:

Yet I know that good is coming to me—that good is always coming;
though few have at all times the simplicity and the courage to believe it. What we call evil is the only and best shape which, for the
person and his condition at the time, could be assumed by the best
good. And so, *Farewell.*

Phantastes is a singular and peculiar tale, sometimes disjointed
in plot and written in a style that varies from the sublime to the
sophomoric. Its evil tree-spirits make it seem like a children's story,
while the young man's encounters with temptresses and tender-
hearted maids give it an air of adolescent romance. But there are
spiritual meditations throughout the story, ruminations on joy and
sorrow, faith and despair, which are clearly the product of a ma-
ture philosophic mind.

Whatever its peculiarities, *Phantastes* was for Lewis a great balm
to the soul, not only in his youth but throughout his lifetime. In his
preface to the MacDonald anthology which he edited two decades
later, Lewis wrote that he "crossed a great frontier" when he first
read *Phantastes,* that the book had about it "a sort of cool, morning innocence, and also, quite unmistakeably, a certain quality of
Death, *good* Death. What it actually did to me was to convert, even
to baptise (that is where the Death came in) my imagination."

The older Lewis did not mistake this kind of baptism for conversion itself, yet recognized it as the beginning of a long process. As
he explained it, *Phantastes* "did nothing to my intellect nor (at that
time) my conscience. Their turn came far later and with the help of
many other books and men. But when the process was complete,
. . . I found that I was still with MacDonald and that he had accompanied me all the way." Only after that process was complete
could Lewis fully explain what he had found so compelling in that
first reading: "The quality which had enchanted me in his imaginative works turned out to be the quality of the real universe, the di-

vine, magical, terrifying, and ecstatic reality in which we all live."

Yet, as Lewis himself would later recognize, the reading of *Phantastes* was only one stage in a pilgrimage that would last many years. Soon after finishing the MacDonald book, seventeen-year-old Jack decided that, as he had been immersing himself in so many tales of adventure and enchantment, it was time for him to try his own hand at it. In the spring and summer of 1916 he composed a sixty-four-page manuscript called "The Quest of Bleheris."

Lewis's only reader at the time was Arthur Greeves, with whom he shared a mutual enthusiasm for northern myths and tales of chivalric adventure. And that is just what "Bleheris" is: a chivalric quest narrative that draws on Nordic mythology. But, perhaps unconsciously on Lewis's part, it is also the story of a spiritual journey, a story left unfinished possibly because Lewis's own spiritual quest was far from resolved.

The "Quest" fragment is the story of Bleheris, a twenty-three-year-old man who has spent his whole life in the "City of Nesses," a town built on a wide bay where rocky slopes plunge down to the sea. When we first meet Bleheris, he is almost a young Don Quixote, trying to live out the romance and adventure he has read about in books. His mother urges him to court the favor of one Lady Alice, the most sought after young woman in the city. And so he dutifully courts her and writes her passionate poems, though he doesn't really feel passion in his heart. When he kisses her, instead of rapture, he feels that her lips are as cold as the grave, and her eyes seem as calm and detached as those of an angel in a stained-glass window.

When Bleheris learns from his mother that his marriage to "Alice the Saint" has been arranged, he feels depressed rather than exultant, deciding that he does not have the proper feeling because he has not yet proven himself or made a name in the world. He vows to set forth on a quest, hoping that he will learn to love her once he is worthy, and so return to make her his bride.

As he is weighing these matters in his mind, Bleheris gazes out the window one moonlit night and contemplates the Great Mountains to the north. Suddenly he feels the exultation that had been missing before. He looks and sees "how stark and grim and baleful they lay in the pale moonlight," which fills him with "a host of memories of all the old tales concerning them—of hideous passes among them, of wizard cities and evil places in their gloomy woods and of knights' adventurings there and in the unheard of lands beyond." The more he peers out and ponders, the more "the dull, sober world in which he lived waxed ever more and more irksome to him" as he compares his heroic ambitions to the mundane realities that most likely await him. He fears he will marry, have children, grow old and feeble, always with a burden of buried dreams. In the midst of these somber musings, though, the moonlit vista spread before his eyes suddenly overpowers him with an entirely different mood: "But even as thus he pondered, those dark moonlit hills with all their wonders were weaving a spell about him: so anon a new thought, as it had been a gust of sweet, cold morning-wind, smote upon the dungeon of his soul, and he almost laughed for joy."

The last word in this passage—*joy*—is, of course, one that would resonate throughout all of Lewis's writings. Here we find his first attempt in fiction to evoke that unique blend of wonder, delight and longing that would become one of the defining experiences of his life. And here too we find so many of the elements associated with Joy: the severe beauty of a moonlit landscape; the distant hills; the lure of uncharted realms and untold adventures; the heart-breaking contrast between the wonders of enchantment and the mundane realities of the everyday world. In later years, once Lewis had returned to faith, he would feel assured he knew what all this meant: that it was the soul's longing to find some lost home and to enter in yet again. In 1916, however, the young agnostic Lewis could only record the experience without claiming to know its meaning.

Once he has decided to go on a journey, Bleheris goes to Alice's father, Sir Lionel, and explains that he would like to put off the wedding because he is a "deedless man" who has not yet earned the right to her hand. When Lionel hears Bleheris's knightly ambitions, he talks over several possible quests, east, west and south. But the magnet for Bleheris's imagination is the North. When Sir Lionel explains that "northward beyond the Mountains a great way is the STRIVER," Bleheris breaks in and asks who this STRIVER is, where he may be found and how he got his name. Lionel answers that men know little of the STRIVER, because the journey to the North is "full evil and bitter," that it is "utter madness" to try and cross the Great Mountains—but that they are only the foothills of even more towering peaks in the lands further on. Lionel says that some consider STRIVER "a monster and a fiend whom men seek to slay," but that an old man who had journeyed to that country and returned "spake of him more as a saint or a god."

Bleheris needs to hear nothing more, and he vows to seek out "him that men call STRIVER" and never to stray from his quest. He reaches this decision in an instant, for since the moment "when first that name fell from the knight's lips, it pierced straightly into his very heart, as something heard a great time past before he was born: and it seemed to him that all things were nothing worth, save only to seek out that One." Clearly, the very name itself evokes a sense of the numinous, with an effect very similar to the name Aslan on the Pevensie children when they first hear it in *The Lion, the Witch, and the Wardrobe.*

Before setting out on his quest, Bleheris goes to the local priest, Father Ulfin, who gives him a flask of holy water to ward off evil. Here the narrator pauses for a bit of intrusive commentary: "Poor boy! that deemed in his folly that a priest's bauble, a dream-thing woven out of the hopes of man's self and then called 'holy,' might avail him aught against the great and terrible powers of the earth."

When Lewis sent the first installment of "Bleheris" to Arthur, the latter apparently objected to this sardonic aside. In a note written in July 1916, Jack said he was sorry if his friend disapproved of such remarks, explaining that it was not Christianity itself he was making fun of but rather the religious practices of a superstitious old priest like Ulfin and a naive young man like Bleheris. Lewis added, however, that Greeves probably would be even more unhappy with the main gist of the story, which would never be stated openly, but embedded in the narrative.

Actually, considering the vehemence of Lewis's letters on Christianity quoted earlier, the wonder is not that the story contains satirical comments about religion, but that it contains so few of them. Lewis's caustic remark about the folly of sacred talismans in "Bleheris" is about what one would expect of a young man raised as an Ulster Protestant and trained in philosophy by an ardent freethinker.

Ironically, Lewis's portraits of church officials in his fiction became more pointed, not less so, once he had rejoined the community of faith. One can find much more biting satire in Lewis's "Christian" books than in his juvenilia. There is the two-faced Steward in *The Pilgrim's Regress,* who lays out an impossible set of rules for John, threatens him with damnation and then winks and tells John not to fret about it. Then there is "Mad Parson" Straik in *That Hideous Strength* (1945), who employs biblical phrases and imagery to preach his heretical gospel of violence and coercive collectivism. In *Till We Have Faces* (1956), the first priest of Ungit reminds us of Father Ulfin, with his blind adherence to superstitious rites; but his young successor, who tries to "demythologize" the blood-stained old traditions, errs in the opposite direction, trying to reduce all religious truths to mere rational self-interest. It would seem that the older, Christian Lewis was much more perturbed by "blind guides" in the church than was the younger, agnostic one.

As Bleheris's story continues, he sets out on his quest, ascending the Cloudy Pass, passing through the Sunken Wood and coming eventually to the Hostel of the Crossways. There he dismounts and goes inside, where he encounters three men of distinctly different appearance. On the left is a tall and gaunt fellow with feverish eyes, a hoarse voice and bony hands that tremble as he speaks. He identifies himself as Gerce the Desirous, who seeks for Tomorrow. On the right is a richly dressed lad of about twenty, "small and light of limb as a girl," who has black, curly hair hanging down in lovelocks. His skin is smooth as porcelain, his voice low and sweet, but he speaks with a melancholy air and keeps his eyes half-closed as if he is "ever dreaming on some age-old pitiful memory." He identifies himself as Wan Jadis, who seeks after Yesterday. Sitting between these two is Hyperites, a robust man of middle years with a full, golden beard and a "cheerful and open countenance."

Before the newcomer has a chance to speak, Hyperites reveals that Bleheris is seeking STRIVER. At this, the young pilgrim simply stares in wonder, speechless with awe. When the excitable Gerce accuses Hyperites of sorcery, the latter answers serenely, "I am but the servant of him they call the STRIVER, to do his will and draw men unto him."

In his brief discussion of the Bleheris manuscript, Lewis's biographer George Sayer has identified Hyperites as a Christ figure, and it is not difficult to see why. He is the servant of the numinous being Bleheris seeks, and his words echo several statements of Jesus quoted in the Gospel of John (6:38-44; 12:49). The name Hyperites suggests the Greek prefix meaning "over" or "above." Hyperites' words seem especially suited to his name, which is akin to the Greek phrase meaning "one who assists."

Before he and Bleheris have exchanged many words, the contentious Gerce breaks in and admonishes the young knight to beware of Hyperites. He goes on to say that if Bleheris ever found the STRIVER, he would indeed require the help of the gods. The young pilgrim crosses himself and insists there is but one God. At this, Gerce pounds the table with his fist, speaking to Bleheris as if he were a wayward child. He says it doesn't matter which of the old beliefs is most true since none can help—either God or the gods—once one falls into the hands of enchanters and sorcerers.

Hyperites again answers calmly, saying that he will bear such charges against himself and his master because he knows Gerce is genuinely concerned about Bleheris. But then he says the real danger is for those like Gerce who seek after Tomorrow, only to be "spilled on the rock Mothlight" and perish in their quest.

"I must take my chance," answers Gerce, "for the Glory that is beyond."

Though he never becomes a fully developed character, Gerce offers an intriguing hint of how early Lewis made up his mind about utopian schemers who propose that humanity save itself through its own efforts. Gerce's lack of composure and his sheer bad manners clearly reveal him to be one whose earnest philosophy has brought him neither peace nor wisdom. He cannot live in the present and shows little interest in the past, so he has developed some vague ideology which will bring about redemption in the future.

Though the unfinished tale never reveals what sort of Tomorrow Gerce had in mind, there is little doubt that the young Lewis did not look to such fanatical utopianists for salvation. The word *Gerce* means "moth or worm" in French, so it is especially ominous that Hyperites sees him perishing by Mothlight, a fluttering creature destroyed by the glowing vision which so attracts him.

Readers of Lewis meet a similar character in a novel written two decades later, *Out of the Silent Planet*. There another rough-hewn visionary, the scientist Edward Weston, proposes to spread humanity from world to world and star to star and so achieve a kind of godhead, even if it means destroying other species—or the members of the human species who are unfit, or unwilling, to join his scheme. In his speech to the governing spirit of Malacandra, Weston defends even mass extermination in the name of the proposed benefits for coming generations. Whereas Gerce remarks laconically, "I must take my chance for the Glory that is beyond," Weston expands on the thought: "I may fall, but while I live I will not, with such a key in my hand, consent to close the gates of the future on my race. What lies in the future, beyond our present ken, passes imagination to conceive: it is enough for me that there is a Beyond."

Some readers of the Ransom trilogy, including J. B. S. Haldane, the Marxist polemicist who may have been the model for Edward Weston, have assumed that Lewis's satirical portrayal of ruthless social engineers is rooted in traditional tensions between the communities of faith and science. But it is clear from the "Bleheris" fragment that Lewis's distrust of ideologues who propose to save humanity from itself predates his adult conversion by more than a decade.

Lewis himself observed that he was ripe for just such an ideology during his Great Bookham years and surmised that it was romanticism, not Christianity, that prevented him from moving further in that direction. In *Surprised by Joy* he expresses his surprise that he was never drawn to "that opposite orthodoxy," that he did not become "a Leftist, Atheist, satiric Intellectual of the type we all know so well." He adds that he had the requisite debunking spirit for the role, but that his Romantic leanings, his attentiveness to the call of Joy, seems to have insulated him from the more hard-edged ideologues. He notes as well that his habitual pessimism about improving the world by human effort seems also to have dampened the appeal of any radical social programs.

Yet if romanticism might save one from the excesses of revolutionary fervor, it might also lead to perils of its own. As Bleheris's adventures continue, he learns that those who seek Yesterday may be every bit as dangerous as those who seek Tomorrow. Afraid that Hyperites might indeed be an enchanter and put off by Gerce's fierce demeanor, the young man turns to reconsider Wan Jadis: "Now the change from the Desirous to the sweet and comely youth was as honey after wormwood or spring after winter: although, in truth, there was more of the sad loveliness of Autumn than of the lustiness of Spring in him." When Bleheris asks Wan Jadis about the place he seeks, his reply weaves its own kind of enchantment. "Ah! The land of Yesterday," he explains dreamily. "It lies in the West, in the times of the setting sun. . . . It is the home of things past, and of all old, forgotten, unhappy memories: a vallied land, full of soft mists and trees that ever shed their leaves in the drowsy winds." He goes on to say that Yesterday is a place where "the queens of olden song abide," women such as Guinevere and Helen of Troy continuing "deathless forever in their sorrow and loveliness." He describes it as a place where one can leave behind the cares and tempests of this world, retreating to a land of "noble sorrow softened by many years."

This halcyon reverie certainly evokes romanticism as the youthful Lewis understood it. Apart from echoing Wordsworth's line about "old, unhappy, far-off things," it also calls to mind the great tragic heroines of myth and legend whose stories Jack and Arthur knew so well. In *Surprised by Joy* Lewis would later explain that the "Idea of Autumn" was one of the main catalysts for those youthful experiences of piercing delight he came to know as Joy.

Wan Jadis seems to be the very embodiment of the "sad loveliness of Autumn." His words weave a spell that makes Bleheris decide to abandon his quest for STRIVER and to seek instead the Land of Yesterday. The young pilgrim fears some silent reproach from Hyperites for this change of plans, but Hyperites does not intervene. He says his task is not to draw men to STRIVER, as he had misspoken earlier, but only to show them the road once they began to seek it on their own. He says he would not bar Bleheris from his quest, even if he thought it might lead to Mothlight. After this somber warning, Hyperites ends the conversation on a more hopeful note, predicting the two of them will meet again before long. He declares that he will always stand ready if the pilgrim decides to resume his original quest.

It is clear from this passage that Hyperites has a solemn respect for the free will of others, even if it leads them to their own destruction. But Hyperites also offers hope that the choices of sincere seekers will eventually lead them back to the right path. Writing thirty years later in *The Great Divorce* (1946), Lewis, by then a Christian, continued to stress the sanctity of free will, stressing both the horrors and the hopes that are the final consequence of one's choices: "There are only two kinds of people in the end: those who say to God, 'Thy will be done,' and those to whom God says, in the end, '*Thy* will be done.' All that are in Hell, choose it."

At this point in his pilgrimage, Bleheris's choice is to follow Wan Jadis, and the two of them bid farewell to Gerce and Hyperites and depart from the Hostel of the Crossways. They journey for many miles until they come to a dark valley of mournful winds and fluttering golden leaves, where their way is blocked by a gray marsh. They find a small boat, called a shallop, tied to a rosebush and set out over the water in heavy mists. Though the marsh seems to Bleheris little more than a slimy bog, Wan Jadis grandiosely calls it a "Sea" upon which they will "sail to Yesterday." Eventually they see a "vast and awful temple" looming ahead in the mists and a withered old crone wearing a gray shroud.

Just then the mud starts oozing in over the sides of the skiff, which founders in the swampy waters; Wan Jadis is sucked into the bog, with water spiders crawling over his handsome, sad face as his head disappears beneath the mud. Bleheris is saved when he is clutched by the branches of the rosebush, which draw him back to the shore from which the boat set out. At first he is angry to feel his cloak torn and his arms scratched by that thorny embrace, but then he recognizes his narrow escape, and he comforts himself, "joying in the coolness and fragrance" of the rose petals. Suddenly, the rosebush appears to him as a lovely woman, her body covered only by her luxuriant, long hair, who reaches out to him with manacled arms, as if pleading for help.

When the vision vanishes, leaving Bleheris weary and alone, he can think of nothing else to do but trudge back to the Hostel of the Crossways. There he finds Gerce still badgering Hyperites, for, as the narrator explains, "Poor Gerce strove often in his speech with every man." But Hyperites tolerates this with good grace, since he pities the Desirous, "seeing the twisted soul, and the pain of this man, and how he lived unsatisfied and ill at ease." When Bleheris recounts his adventures at the Gray Marsh, Gerce weeps at the loss of Wan Jadis and argues that it was the Rose, not the STRIVER, who had drawn Bleheris to the quest that had almost cost him his life. "Yet many have come to Him by way of the Rose," answers Hyperites, "Or rather they so used ere she was led captive. Her spirit, I think, must have sickened in the long years of bondage."

Bleheris's excursion to the Gray Marsh seems as fraught with allegory as any passage in *The Pilgrim's Regress.* Lewis added a note to Arthur on the "Bleheris" manuscript explaining that the old woman at the temple is modeled on Hela, the goddess of the underworld in Nordic mythology. Wan Jadis, whose name combines the word for "pale" with the French adjective for "times of yore," is one whose search for Joy has become effete and sentimental, leading not to yesterday, but to death. (The powerful witch Jadis whom we meet in *The Magician's Nephew* is nothing like this pallid aesthete; yet she too comes from a world where death prevails.)

The Rose at one end of the Gray Marsh is a more ambiguous symbol than the temple at the other end. One cannot help but wonder about the connection with *Phantastes,* the beech-tree maid, who is such a comfort to Anodos. The young Lewis's Rosemaid evokes some of the same pathos—and also eros. She seems to represent the spirit of romance, whom the young Lewis had encountered so often in his favorite texts from the twelfth century to the nineteenth, but who seemed fettered in his own generation.

At the time he wrote "Bleheris," Lewis was still confused about the connection between the romantic impulse and the religious impulse; he was also uncertain about the nature of Joy, which seemed to evoke both the numinous and the amorous. In his commentary on "Bleheris," George Sayer observes that the tale is "most obviously a quest for the deity and for the feminine, the two not necessarily at variance with each other." Though they may not be at variance, it was essential for Lewis's spiritual pilgrimage that he learn to distinguish between them. The two sides of the young Lewis's dilemma are expressed perfectly by Gerce, who debunks the quest for STRIVER as really only a search for the Rose, and by Hyperites, who answers that many have found him by way of the Rose.

Hyperites's response anticipates exactly the argument developed later in *The Pilgrim's Regress,* where Reason explains that all human loves are mere copies of the more perfect divine love. In his preface to the same book, Lewis explores more fully the relation between religion and romance. To those who would deride romanticism as "spilt religion," Lewis answers that he accepts that label, agreeing that "he who has religion ought not to spill it." But he adds that the golden drops, though spilled, may form a trail which one can follow back to the Source. That is, one's inner sense of glory and gratitude for all that is beautiful and sublime may be the first step on a road to faith.

But if Lewis already sensed a link between his romanticism and religious faith by the time he was seventeen, he was still far from resolving the issue. It seems that at this point in the manuscript, Lewis began to lose the thread of the story. In June of 1916, he wrote to Arthur, "I think Bleheris has killed my muse—always rather a sickly child." And indeed the tale begins to unravel after Bleheris returns to the Hostel of the Crossways. First he meets a massive, ominous figure with the melodious name Bethrelladoom, an enemy of Hyperites. Then he receives a message from Father Ulfin that Alice has run away to the northern city of Ralholt. The young knight adds a squire to his retinue, one Nut, son of Nut, and continues his journey north, both to renew his quest for STRIVER and to seek the now less-than-saintly Alice.

Ralholt is a great seaport and royal city, similar in description to Cair Paravel in the Narnia Chronicles. What strikes Bleheris as most unusual about Ralholt is that a magnificent Christian cathedral and an equally splendid temple of Odin stand side by side in the heart of the city, for it is a place where Christians and those of other religions live in peace and harmony, "being too busied in their daily lives to waste their strength in shadowy things."

As the story trails off into hastily sketched characters and undeveloped episodes, Hyperites continues to be the most intriguing figure in the narrative. At one point Bleheris draws his sword when Gerce mocks his God, but when Hyperites bids them be at peace, they obey, for as the narrator explains, "They both feared and loved this servant of the STRIVER." Later Bleheris discovers that, from the house servant Nut to the king of the realm, everyone holds Hyperites in the same high esteem and considers him a personal friend. The reader too is drawn to this character, without ever learning who he is or what his eventual fate might have been. The reverence he inspires far outweighs the ridicule directed at a conventional religious figure like Father Ulfin.

But if Lewis seemed willing to travel further in his imagination than in his intellect, eventually his imagination faltered. The manuscript ends abruptly on page sixty-four, soon after Bleheris arrives at Ralholt. In the same letter to Greeves in which he argued that all religions were human inventions—Christ as much as Loki—Jack also announced: "As to Bleheris, he is dead and I shan't trouble his grave." In 1916 Lewis's imagination was suggesting that Christian myth and Nordic myth could be venerated equally, while his intellect was telling him they could be dismissed equally. Not able to rest in either conclusion, Lewis would continue to grapple with this issue throughout his teens and twenties.

In "Bleheris," the seventeen-year-old Lewis revealed how far he had come in his personal quest—and how far he had yet to go. At that age he could eloquently describe the experience of Joy, but he did not claim to understand it. By then he also recognized the opposite dangers of an arid reductionism on the one hand and a self-indulgent romanticism on the other. Most intriguing of all is his portrayal of an elusive god figure whose servant goes among the people, befriending all and making peace among them, seeking to draw them to his master.

Yet what reality did the experience of Joy point to? When would reason, revelation and romanticism ever speak with one accord? And how could the beautiful dreams of myth and story ever be reconciled to the grim actualities of the waking world? Lewis would be nearly twice as old before he felt able to weave a coherent worldview from these tangled skeins.

FIVE

DUALISM DURING THE WAR YEARS

By the time he was twenty, Lewis was a wounded war veteran and a published poet. By then he had also developed an emotional attachment to the woman who would serve as his adoptive mother, sharing his household for nearly three decades. Lewis once wrote that "youth and age touch only the surface of our lives," and this seems especially true of Jack himself. If he would prove surprisingly youthful in later years, publishing the Narnia Chronicles in his fifties, he was, at age twenty, one of the oldest young men of that scarred and disheartened generation.

During the years of the Great War, and immediately after, Lewis continued to ponder the relation of matter and spirit. His mind was not able to rest on pure materialism, for radical skepticism too often contradicted itself. Nor did it explain his moments of Joy and the elusive otherworlds they seemed to evoke. In the short term his war experiences seemed to reinforce in him a kind of gnostic dualism, an eternal opposition of matter and spirit. But the longer he stayed at Oxford, the more he explored varieties of spiritualism and Idealism, in which things unseen were believed to be more fundamental than those which could be seen.

Lewis entered University College, Oxford, in the last week of April 1917, after his examiner proclaimed his entrance examinations the best he'd ever seen. This is not surprising considering the rigorous tutoring offered by William Kirkpatrick, who himself wrote to Albert Lewis that Jack was the most accomplished student he had ever tutored in his entire teaching career. The week after he moved into his rooms at "Univ," Jack also enrolled in the Officers' Training Corps. By the spring of 1917, World War I was well into its third year, and Jack seems to have felt honor-bound to join the fight. As an Irish resident he could have avoided military service in the British army, but since he had been attending English schools since the age of nine, he seems to have assumed it was his duty to serve the country that had become his adopted homeland.

In June 1917 Lewis joined a cadet battalion for formal training and was billeted at Keble College, also in Oxford. His roommate at Keble was Edward F. C. "Paddy" Moore, who introduced Jack to his mother, Mrs. Janie King Moore, then forty-five, and his eleven-year-old sister, Maureen. Lewis took an immediate liking to Paddy and his family, feeling a sense of belonging with them that had been so often missing during his boyhood and adolescence.

During his two years of military service, Jack in effect exchanged parents, gaining a new mother and all but losing his father. When he received a month's leave from mid-September to mid-October, Lewis spent the first three weeks with the Moore family at their home in Bristol, leaving only a week to visit his father in Belfast.

After returning to England to join his regiment, Jack was ordered to the front on November 15, after a forty-eight-hour leave.

That did not leave enough time to cross over to Ireland and back, so he wired his father, asking for a rendezvous in Bristol. Albert apparently did not understand the telegram and did not visit Jack, who crossed the Channel with his battalion, the First Somerset Light Infantry, arriving on the front lines on his nineteenth birthday, November 29.

Trench fighting in France was, of course, a nightmare beyond description, and the experience seems to have influenced Lewis's philosophical outlook for several years after the war. In *Surprised by Joy* Lewis touches on the topic only briefly, but the images he offers are unforgettable. He speaks of trenches knee-deep in water, of vast, cratered landscapes where not even a blade of grass had survived, of mutilated soldiers on the battlefield "still moving like half-crushed beetles," of corpses frozen in a sitting position.

Jack's first few months on the front were relatively quiet, with no direct assaults or repulses along his section of the line. In February 1918 he developed a case of trench fever and spent the whole month in a hospital at Le Tréport. After rejoining his battalion for another three weeks of relative quiet, he was one of several hundred thousand British and Commonwealth troops who bore the brunt of the final German attack on the Western front. He was in an active theater of combat for three weeks, until April 15, when an English shell fell short, killing his regimental sergeant and wounding him in three places—the back of his left hand, his thigh just above the knee and his left side below the armpit. Lewis was to carry this experience with him for the rest of his life—including a piece of shrapnel lodged in his chest which was not removed until 1944, when it seemed to be working its way dangerously close to his heart.

Borne off the field by stretcher-bearers, Jack was sent first to a mobile hospital in Étaples, France. When Warren, a captain in the

Royal Army Service Corps, heard the news, he borrowed a bicycle and rode fifty miles within the sound of the guns in order to be with his brother.

By contrast, Albert Lewis seemed strangely passive during his son's ordeal. When Jack was shipped back across the Channel to a hospital in London, he telegraphed his father late in April and asked that he come visit him during his convalescence. Albert replied that he couldn't travel because he was suffering from bronchitis (though his diaries from that month show he was going to work every day). In June the younger Lewis wrote his father, "I know that you will come and see me," adding that he was "never before so eager to cling to every bit of our old home life and see you." Jack admitted that he had not always been the best of sons, but concluded, "Please God, I shall do better in the future. Come and see me. I am homesick, that is the long and short of it."

Still Albert did not come. He was wedded to his work and had an almost pathological aversion about any departure from his daily routine. There is no doubt that he dearly loved his son, but he seemed to believe he could offer the needed emotional support by post. Mrs. Moore, though, did make the trip, and Jack reported to his father that he and Mrs. Moore had "seen a good deal of each other" and that she had "certainly been a very, very good friend to me."

During that summer Mrs. Moore was in even greater straits than the patient she was visiting. In late March her son Paddy had been reported missing in action and, after five agonizing months, it was confirmed that he was dead. Throughout the spring and summer of 1918, the bereaved mother and the abandoned son turned to each other for strength and consolation.

Though it is doubtful that any further bond was needed, Jack and Paddy pledged before they were shipped off to France that if one of them did not return from the fighting, the other would do his best to look after the parent left behind. (For readers who wonder about the credibility of two teenage boys promising to look after the other's middle-aged parent, it should be noted that Paddy's sister, Maureen, overhead this conversation and confirmed what was said. In addition, Mrs. Moore wrote to Albert Lewis in October 1918, "Jack has been so good to me. My poor son asked him to look after me if he did not come back. He possesses for his age such a wonderful power of understanding and sympathy.")

In July Lewis was strong enough to be moved to a convalescent hospital. When he learned that none was available in northern Ireland, he selected one in Clifton, Bristol, near the home of Mrs. Moore. He continued to write his father requesting a visit, but by autumn his letters had changed from plaintive to sardonic. On October 3 he wrote to Albert, "It is four months now since I returned from France, and my friends laughingly suggest that 'my father in Ireland' of whom they hear is a mythical creation."

Later that month, when Jack was transferred to the Officers' Command Depot in Eastbourne, Sussex, Mrs. Moore and Maureen took lodgings near the camp in order to be near Jack. By the time the Armistice was declared and Jack was demobilized, his home was where Mrs. Moore and Maureen were, while Albert's house outside Belfast was a place for brief, strained visits on holiday, usually arranged to coincide with times when Warren would be on leave.

The irony of this whole episode is that for several years before the war the boys' complaint about their father was not that he was inattentive but that he was overly attentive. As Warren and Jack grew into young manhood, Albert increasingly turned to them for companionship, but the friendship he offered was not the kind they sought. Writing to Arthur Greeves in 1916, for example, Jack apologizes for not inviting him over to the Lewis household more often during his holidays in Belfast, explaining that his father presented a great obstacle. Jack whimsically suggests that they might have more time to themselves if they poisoned "old Stokes," one of their neighbors, so that Albert could marry the widow.

In his gloss on this letter, Warren speculates that if Arthur had ever paid a visit to Little Lea, Mr. Lewis would have welcomed him cordially, then proceeded to commandeer the conversation, doing nine-tenths of the talking himself, perhaps giving readings from his favorite speeches and essays, not leaving the boys a moment to themselves to talk about their own interests. Both brothers valued the "little end room" in the family homestead precisely because no adult set foot there, not even the housemaids.

In his books Lewis often associates the word *interference* with adults in general, but especially with his father. By contrast, the word *solitude* for him does not connote loneliness, but rather time to oneself, time to read or think or write or draw—in short, freedom from interference. During his stays at home, Jack actually looked forward to Monday mornings when his father would be returning to work and Jack could recover his treasured solitude. It seems a cruel twist that when Lewis sincerely yearned for his father's company, Albert felt incapable of making the trip, not knowing that his son's affections were turning elsewhere.

Though his feelings for Mrs. Moore began as a curious blend of infatuation and filial duty, he and she gradually settled into a straightforward arrangement of adoptive son and mother. Warren Lewis noted that within a year of his return to Oxford, Jack was introducing Mrs. Moore as his mother. About the same time he stopped referring to her as "Mrs. Moore" and began calling her by the affectionate nickname "Minto." As Maureen Moore explained simply, "He had lost his mother in childhood. That is where my mother came in."

Critics and biographers have shown a great deal of interest in whether or not Jack and Mrs. Moore were physically intimate in the early years of their relationship. A. N. Wilson frankly calls them "lovers" and says the burden of proof is on anyone who would say otherwise. Walter Hooper refers to Mrs. Moore as Lewis's "friend and companion" in one of his books, but speculates in another that the two of them may have been intimate. Owen Barfield felt that the chances of a sexual element to the relationship were about fifty-fifty.

Whatever the case, this issue is not one that bears directly on a study of Lewis's spiritual development. Lewis was about as far from faith as he would ever get when he first met Mrs. Moore, and he did not feel at all bound by Christian ethics or conventional mores. Too great an interest in such a question may bear out Lewis's observation in *The Personal Heresy* that readers too often prefer to gossip about the frank details of writers' lives rather than to read their books.

While he was convalescing, Jack put together a collection of poems he'd written, not surprisingly about love and war, but also expressing his personal philosophy at that time. Titled *Spirits in Bondage,* the book was published by William Heinemann in March 1919, under the pseudonym Clive Hamilton, in honor of his deceased mother.

The most haunting poem in the collection is "French Nocturne," a description of a World War I battlefield as evening descends. All is quiet in the darkling trenches, as "the jaws of a sacked village" along the ridge have "swallowed up the sun," leaving only an angry red streak of its blood along the horizon. A lone airplane appears in the dusky sky, seeming to fly straight toward a pale, green moon. For a moment it seems the plane "nears in that white land some harbour of dear dreams." But soon the poet realizes this is but an illusion: "That he's no nearer the

moon than I / And she's a stone that catches the sun's beam."
The poem ends by asking how a soldier can presume to make
poems out of war:

> What call have I to dream of anything?
> I am a wolf. Back to the world again,
> And speech of fellow-brutes that once were men
> Our throats can bark for slaughter: cannot sing.

Lewis later wrote that his war experiences were so surreal and
alien that they were emotionally cut off from the rest of his life. Yet
here again one can sense elements of continuity: the pensive
moonlight scene, the romantic spirit longing for escape to some
other world, but also the rationalist voice who "sees through" it all
and declares the beckoning moon to be only a ball of stone re-
flecting the fading sunlight.

Both these moods seek utterance throughout *Spirits in Bondage,* but it is generally the second, the rationalist, which predomi-
nates. The first section, titled "The Prison House," opens with the
poem "Satan Speaks":

> I am Nature, the Mighty Mother,
> I am the law: ye have none other.
>
> I am the flower and the dewdrop fresh,
> I am the lust in your itching flesh.
>
> I am the battle's filth and strain,
> I am the widow's empty pain.
>
> I am the sea to smother your breath,
> I am the bomb, the falling death.
>
> I am the fact and the crushing reason
> To thwart your fantasy's new-born treason.

I am the spider making her net,
I am the beast with jaws blood-wet.

I am the wolf that follows the sun
And I will catch him ere day is done.

The wolf following the sun in the last stanza is an allusion to
Fenris the Wolf in Norse mythology, a great beast symbolizing destruction and chaos. In some versions Fenris swallows the sun on
Ragnarok, the day of doom, killing even Odin himself, chieftain of
the gods, bringing about the end of the world and the twilight of
the gods. In "Satan Speaks" the wolf image suggests that ultimately
all human aspirations and dreams will come to nought as the
forces of Nature eventually bring an end to our world, its sun and
the human race itself. (This wolf reappears in *The Lion, the Witch,
and the Wardrobe* as Fenris Ulf, head of the White Witch's secret
police. He is slain by Peter the High King in a climactic battle. In
the Christian worldview which informs the Narnia Chronicles,
death and chaos do not ultimately prevail, but rather Aslan and his
followers.)

If "Satan Speaks" gives voice to the brute forces of nature, then
the reader wonders what sort of God the poet looks to for hope or
redemption. But there is no such god to be found for yearning
spirits imprisoned in bonds of flesh. Several other poems in the
collection echo this sentiment. In "De Profundis" the poet declares,
"The good is dead. Let us curse God most High." If there is a "just
God that cares for earthly pain," the poet adds, he is "far away beyond our labouring night." In "Ode for a New Year's Day," the
poet explains that he had once execrated God because evil and
death seem to rule the world, but having grown wiser, he now un-
derstands that "our own hearts have made a phantom called the
Good" which really has nothing to do with a creator who "tosses

the dust of chaos and gives the suns their parts."

When it appeared in 1919, *Spirits in Bondage* descended on the literary world with a gentle thud. There were a few polite reviews, but sales were negligible. The book did create something of a stir in the Lewis family though. When Warren read a typescript of the book, he fretted in a letter to his father that "no useful purpose is served by endeavoring to advertise oneself as an Atheist." Albert reacted more philosophically, replying that "[Jack] is young and will learn in time that a man has not absolutely solved the riddle of the heavens above and the earth beneath and the waters under the earth at twenty. I am not going to slop over but I do think if Oxford does not spoil him . . . he may write something that men would not willingly let die." All the same, when Jack was staying with his father in Belfast, the latter cautioned him about leaving a copy of *Spirits in Bondage* out in plain sight, lest one of the servants pick it up and read it.

Indeed, one is tempted to wonder if the anti-Christian outbursts in *Spirits in Bondage* provided a way for the young Lewis to lash out at Albert and his orthodox opinions. But the elder Lewis had been consulted as the book was taking shape and he even had a hand in choosing its title and Lewis's *nom de plume*. And after the book was published, Jack wrote again to his father, reassuring him that the "God" being denounced in his poems was not the God of Christianity.

The philosophy behind *Spirits in Bondage* is not so much atheism as a kind of gnosticism, a radical dichotomy between the pure world of the spirit and the corrupt world of matter. Writing to Arthur Greeves from the field hospital in Étaples about five weeks after he was wounded, Lewis declared that his views on the "lusts of the flesh" were becoming almost monastic, not because he considered lust sinful but because one shouldn't let Matter, one's

body, dominate Spirit, one's mind. He explained that on the battlefield one witnesses "spirit continually dodging matter (shells, bul-
lets, animal fears, animal pain)," illustrating an eternal opposition
between the higher realm, Beauty, and the lower, which might be
called Matter or Nature or even "Satan."

Apparently this view struck Greeves as rather bleak and life-
denying, for Lewis wrote again a fortnight later, this time from a
hospital in London, defending himself against the claim that, of all
things, he was beginning to sound too much like his father. To this
charge Lewis admits that his newfound philosophy has a streak of
asceticism to it, a kind of "puritan practice without puritan dogma."
But he repeats that he believes in no God, certainly not one who
might punish him for bodily indulgence. His own desire to deny
the flesh, he explains, derives from his gnostic convictions: "I do
believe that I have a spirit, a chip, shall we say, of universal spirit;
and that since all good & joyful things are spiritual & non-material,
I must be careful not to let matter (= nature = Satan, remember) get
too great a hold on me, & dull the one spark I have."

In the same letter Jack also articulates the more positive side of
his new philosophy. He explains that the beauty we see in a tree
does not reside in the tree itself, because in reality it is only "a
combination of colourless, shapeless, invisible atoms." The true
beauty arises out of something spiritual, either the relationship between the tree and the observer, or perhaps from "some indwelling
spirit behind the matter of the tree." From this example, Lewis concludes that Spirit does indeed exist, that we encounter it in the
forms of "thrills," our experiences of the sublime and the beautiful.
He says that Christians are wrong in thinking that Spirit created
Matter. Rather, it is "matter's great enemy: and that Beauty is the
call of the spirit in that something to the spirit in us."

From this letter, it is clear that long before he became a Christian Lewis was already viewing his experiences of Joy as a signpost to some transcendent reality. At that stage he recognized his views as distinctly non-Christian, since there was no place here for an incarnate God who had redeemed the material world. Instead, Lewis at this stage was almost Manichaean, insisting that Spirit and Matter existed in a state of perpetual opposition.

Though Lewis's letters and poems from this period link his somber views to his battlefield experiences, the roots of this philosophy go back a bit further—to his reading of Schopenhauer while still at Great Bookham. In his most influential work, *The World as Will and Idea* (1819), Schopenhauer argues that behind human life there is simply Nothing: our created universe has existed for a specific, finite time, and before that there were only darkness and chaos. The human intellect evolved as a practical tool for meeting daily exigencies and is impotent to penetrate life's deepest realities. Schopenhauer insists that traditional ideas of God, free will and immortality are illusions; the true forces in the cosmos are the unconscious, mechanistic forces of Nature and Will, the self-consciousness of humans. Though it is the natural side of humans that tricks them into perpetuating their species, they must strive to cultivate their spiritual side—consciousness, will—denying the flesh and seeking repose in art, literature and music.

Lewis reread a handbook on Schopenhauer while recovering from his wounds and wrote to Arthur Greeves that the book reminded him of Kirkpatrick, whose "talk was saturated with Schopenhauer-esque quotations and ideas." That characterization would have fit Jack himself equally well during this period of his life. To Greeves he explained the theme of *Spirits in Bondage* to be that "nature is wholly diabolical & malevolent and that God, if he exists, is outside of and in opposition to the cosmic arrangements."

For all its intensity, however, Lewis's Schopenhauer phase was relatively brief. Schopenhauer's ideas are bracing but cheerless. The philosopher was temperamentally a pessimist—as was his latter-day disciple, William Kirkpatrick. Though Jack suffered from bouts of what his brother called "Celtic melancholy," especially during those months of convalescence from his wounds, he was not temperamentally gloomy or fatalistic. It might be easy to view the material world as evil, and flesh as a snare, from a muddy battlefield or a hospital bed. But the conviction seemed less secure in coming months for a young man enjoying Minto's excellent breakfasts, sitting in an Oxford pub with friends or walking the lush green hills of County Down.

In *Surprised by Joy* Lewis notes that his reading of Henri Bergson in 1918 was an important first step in moving away from Schopenhauer. Bergson, says Lewis, showed him "the snares that lurk about the word *Nothing*" and helped him get past Schopenhauer's "haunting idea . . . that the universe might not have existed." The book Lewis has in mind here is *Creative Evolution,* first published in 1907. In it Bergson critiques the notion that the physical universe is a cosmic fluke, that it was preceded at some time eons ago by a pure Void, and that it need not have existed at all.

Bergson argues that we can conceive of an empty glass, as opposed to a full one, by retaining the idea of the glass. And we can conceive of an empty universe, as opposed to one with galaxies, worlds and life forms, only by retaining the idea of a universe, something which exists. To posit the existence of nonexistence is, for Bergson, a logical impossibility. One might assert that a chalk circle is present or absent from a blackboard, but one cannot argue that the *idea* of a circle does not exist, for it is independent of, and logically prior to, any particular physical circle. In the same way, there are logical principles, such as that A = A, which are eternal, self-existing and have no meaningful logical opposites. To Bergson, *existence* itself is such a term, an object necessary for any contemplating subject, regardless of how dark and empty one might try to imagine the universe. For him a nonexistent universe is like a square circle, "a self-destructing idea, a pseudo-idea, a mere word."

Besides his reading, Lewis's new acquaintances at Oxford after the war helped contribute to his spiritual healing, a gradual moving away from his sense that the physical world was "wholly diabolical & malevolent." In 1919 he met Owen Barfield, whom he would later call "the wisest and best of my unofficial teachers." It was Barfield who first brought home to Lewis the problem with any philosophy that saw the physical world as "rock-bottom reality." If one believes that human thought is merely an expression of neural activity, an evolutionary survival tool, then how can one have any confidence in that thought itself? If we are to assume that abstract thinking provides valid insights about external reality, then we cannot be strict empiricists, believing that all truth is ultimately derived from sense impressions of the physical world.

While Barfield offered an intellectual critique of gnostic dualism, other friends like Alfred K. Hamilton Jenkin helped bring about a change that was more emotional and instinctual. Just as Arthur Greeves back in Ireland had taught Jack to appreciate "the Homely"—simple, natural things—Jenkin showed him how to revel in the senses, how to become a "seeing, listening, smelling, receptive creature." In their walking tours around the Oxfordshire countryside, Jenkin would seek out the "very quiddity of the thing," the most dismal wood on a dismal day, even the place of greatest squalor in a squalid town. His sheer enthusiasm for their physical surroundings had a salutary effect on Jack, who was already a Wordsworthian romantic by temperament. Gradually, as nightmare memories of muddy trenches faded, so too did Jack's Schopenhauerian pessimism.

One cannot also help but wonder if Lewis's frequent rereading of *Phantastes* was also continuing to do its work during this period of healing. In 1923 Jack wrote in his diary that he was reading *Phantastes* yet again, that it served almost as a devotional book for him. According to his dualistic philosophy, humans must endeavor, however futilely, to nurture the life of the spirit and turn their backs on the lures of the material world. But in reading MacDonald, "the call of the spirit" took a different form. As Lewis later explained, his earlier "visitation[s] of Joy" left him dissatisfied with our physical world. The beauties of actual clouds or trees seemed only a pale reflection of some more glorious realm. But in reading MacDonald he "saw the bright shadow coming out of the book into the real world and resting there, transforming all common things and yet itself unchanged." This time he felt that ordinary things were not dimmed by the glory but rather burnished by it.

Though the young Lewis was enthralled by *Phantastes* and returned to it over and over again, he did not fully understand at the time a key source of its imaginative power: its Christian affirmation of both spirit and matter, its sense that the physical world is lifted up, redeemed by the work of the cross.

In his midteens Lewis's thinking had been dominated by materialism, a belief that the physical world is the "rock-bottom reality." In his late teens and early twenties his letters and poems express his Schopenhauerian dualism, a sense of unceasing warfare between matter and spirit. As he grew older, Jack came to believe more and more that the bedrock of reality must be sought in the world of the spirit.

The Kirkpatricks

C. S. Lewis in childhood

The Lewis homestead, Little Lea, in 1905

Water-colour and ink drawing of ruins of the first united Boxonian Parliament House in Pisscia, by C. S. Lewis. Early, but not primitive. Rediscovered 1926 and dated conjecturally 1907 (?)

Illustration for the Boxen stories, 1907

Albert Lewis, 1898

Albert, Warren and C. S. Lewis, 1910

Albert and C. S. Lewis, 1917

Lt. Warren Lewis, 1916

C. S. Lewis, Maureen and Mrs. Moore on holiday in Cornwall, 1927

C. S. Lewis after returning from the war, 1919

Owen Barfield

J. R. R. Tolkien in 1911, age nineteen

SIX

"SPIRITUAL LUST" & THE
LURE OF THE OCCULT

Ralph Waldo Emerson wrote that "a foolish consistency is the hobgoblin of little minds." Before Lewis even arrived at Oxford it was clear that he had no little mind—he was already reading in five languages—and also that he was not hampered by any "foolish consistency." For at the same time Jack began espousing materialism, the philosophy that the physical world is all there is, he became increasingly interested in spiritualism and many other speculations about the nonphysical dimensions of reality.

In *Surprised by Joy* Lewis recalls that his materialistic "faith" began to waver toward the end of his stay with Kirkpatrick. In reading literary figures with occult interests, such as William Butler Yeats and Maurice Maeterlinck, he began to contemplate the great "Perhaps," the possibility that there might be a great deal going on in the universe not readily accessible to the senses.

Lewis later recognized the paradox of the radically contradictory views he was entertaining at the same time. In *Surprised by Joy* he explains that his atheistic convictions and his occult speculations swayed him in different moods, both serving equally to insulate him against Christian faith.

In an unpublished autobiographical fragment composed about 1930, Lewis explains more fully that his simultaneous attraction to materialism and spiritualism was less a matter of contradiction than of oscillation, his restless spirit swinging like a pendulum between opposite extremes. He goes on to say that during his later teens there was an ongoing tension between his "settled view of life," that there was nothing beyond the physical realm, and his hungry imagination, which habitually fed on pictures of other worlds and unseen beings. Every few months this tension would become so great that he allowed himself a brief "magical excursion," some reading or experiment "in the spookical direction." All of his occult explorations followed the same pattern: first there would be "a fine debauch of excitement," then a return of childhood fears about ghosts and bogeys, ending by his "scampering back into the friendly arms of a safe, homely materialism."

The world of seances, paranormal phenomena and occult traditions seemed, at first look, to offer Jack some middle ground between an arid atheism and an oppressive orthodoxy. If materialism were true, then the whole world of his imagination and Joy was mere childish escapism, and he needed to build his philosophy, as he would later quote Bertrand Russell, "upon a firm foundation of unshakable despair." But neither did he wish to return to those sleepless nights at Wynyard when the spiritual demands of Christianity seemed to bear down on him like that blazing full moon. Spiritualism seemed to offer many of the consolations of religion without its obligations. One might take comfort in the possibility of life after death, the assurance that one's lost loved ones had survived in another world, without shouldering the burdens of orthodox belief or the guilt of repeated moral failure.

As mentioned in chapter three, the seeds for Lewis's later interest in the occult were planted back in his Cherbourg days by that good-hearted but spiritually unfocused matron, who was "floundering in the mazes of theosophy, Rosicrucianism, Spiritualism, the whole Anglo-American Occultist tradition." Rosicrucianism, a fraternal order of mystical and metaphysical teachings, dates back to fifteenth-century Germany. Though its specific teachings are shrouded in secrecy, Rosicrucianism, or "The Order of the Rosy Cross," began as an attempt to blend the study of alchemy with the more mystical teachings of Christianity, focusing not only on the transmutation of grosser metals into gold but also on transforming the grosser human qualities into the higher ones.

Theosophy is a general term for occult studies, whose origins are often associated with the seventeenth-century German mystic Jacob Boehme. In recent times the word has been linked more specifically with the Theosophical Society, founded in 1875 by a flamboyant Russian woman named Helena Blavatsky. Madame Blavatsky, as she styled herself, wrote a series of books about ancient religions and occult lore, giving her own version of how humanity and spirituality have evolved through the centuries. In her world tours, she also amazed audiences with her performance as a spirit medium, summoning her "spooks," as she called them, to reveal the secret thoughts of her listeners. She also offered new revelations about life beyond death, as revealed to her by a Tibetan spirit master named Koot-Hoomi.

Blavatsky had a profound influence on the Irish poet William Butler Yeats (1865-1939), who in turn seems to have been the main catalyst for Lewis's interest in spiritualism. For Jack it was an utter novelty to encounter someone he considered an educated, respectable writer who, though not a Christian, rejected materialism out of hand and took the practice of magic quite seriously and literally. (*Magic,* in this context, of course, does not refer to entertainers who perform sleight-of-hand tricks. It alludes rather to necromancers or spiritualists who claim to have contact with the dead or to call on occult forces.)

Another author who stimulated Jack's interest in the occult was Maurice Maeterlinck (1862-1947), a Belgian dramatist and essayist. Now remembered mainly for his symbolic children's fantasy *The Blue Bird,* Maeterlinck was considered a major literary figure in his own generation, winning the Nobel Prize in 1911. Maeterlinck's plays were often imbued with mystical overtones, and in his later years he wrote explicitly about his interest in spiritualism and the occult. Perhaps his most influential and controversial book was *The Great Secret* (1912), in which he flatly stated that Christianity was unsatisfactory as an answer to spiritual questions. Maeterlinck recommended instead the exotic speculations of Zoroastrian sun worshipers, Chaldean astrologers, the Egyptian cult of Osiris, the alchemists of pre-Socratic Greece and the Jewish Kabbala. Maeterlinck seemed to feel that valuable spiritual insights could be obtained from just about every tradition *except* Christianity. (His friend and biographer, Patrick Mahony, suggests that this attitude may be related to his boyhood education at a Jesuit school in St. Barbe, which Maeterlinck called the "Seven Years' Tyranny" and which Mahony says "scarred his mind for life.")

Apart from literary influences, Lewis was also intensely interested during his late teens in more "scientific" approaches to the paranormal. In the summer of 1917 he studied William Fletcher Barrett's *Psychical Research* (1911) and recommended it to his friend Arthur Greeves, adding, "The phenomena are certainly extraordinary, tho' I fear they do not actually prove the agency of real spirits—yet." About the same time Jack was also reading Frederick W. H. Myers's *Science and a Future Life* (1893) and Sir Oliver J. Lodge's *Raymond, or Life and Death* (1916).

All these explorers of the paranormal were associated with the Society for Psychical Research, founded in 1882. If Madame Blavatsky's Theosophical Society presented spirit manifestations as a new kind of revealed religion, the SPR proposed to study these phenomena as scientific subjects. For most of the nineteenth century the prestige and influence of science had been growing, while that of traditional religion had been on the decline. In the closing decades of that century and the opening decades of the next, there was a kind of twilight period in which serious scientific minds wondered if "supernormal phenomena," as they called it—hypnotic trances, spirit mediums, ouija boards, divining rods and so on—could perhaps be studied using the methods of empirical research.

Among the founders of the Society for Psychical Research, Barrett and Lodge were both Fellows of the Royal Society. Other members included physicist Madame Marie Curie, philosopher Henri Bergson, government leaders such as A. J. Balfour and William Gladstone, and writers such as Alfred, Lord Tennyson, and John Ruskin. Also interested in the work of the Society were French psychologist Pierre Janet, who coined the term "dissociation" to describe altered personality states, and American psychologist and philosopher William James.

Frederick W. H. Myers's *Science and a Future Life* was a pioneering study for psychic researchers. In this book he argues that materialist science has dismissed the possibility of life after death because of "the obvious fact that, when a man dies, you hear nothing more from him." Yet Myers goes on to examine telepathy, clairvoyance and apparitions of the dead, arguing that human consciousness is not entirely contained in the physical body, and that these phenomena would eventually become recognized by science as the practice of hypnotism had become.

Sir Oliver Lodge's *Raymond, or Life After Death* offers one particular case study, the attempts of the author to contact his dead son, Raymond, who had been killed during World War I. Early on, Lodge says he will present "the facts" concerning life after death and that he has had "direct experience" of communicating with the dead. But as the case unfolds, one finds a great deal of interpretation and qualification, suggesting that spiritualists, like other believers, must learn to walk by faith, not by sight.

For example, Lodge announces that he was warned by a spirit medium that his son would die in battle. The reader may picture a scene in which Lodge attends a seance and hears a grim prophecy such as "I'm very sorry to tell you this, sir, but your son will be killed near Ypres later this week." But what actually happened was that a medium in Boston told a friend of Lodge's, amid an hour's worth of cryptic messages, to "remember Faunus and the poet." The friend asked Lodge, back in England, if this meant anything to him, and Lodge scoured his classical library until he found a scene in which the poet Horace says a tree almost blew down on him, but the god Faunus warded off the blow. Lodge interpreted this to mean that he or someone close to him was in danger, but that his "Helpers" on the other side would protect him.

Later that week Lodge found out his son had been killed in battle; he consulted Latin scholars and discovered that Faunus hadn't actually warded off the blow of the falling tree, only deflected it to keep it from being a crushing blow. Lodge saw this as a prophecy that his Helpers would keep him from being crushed by grief, reminding him that "love reaches beyond the Chasm." Lodge also believed that this message had come from none other than his former colleague at the SPR, Frederick Myers (who had died in

1901), acting as a "control" on the other side, a medium in the spirit world who helped departed souls contact the living through mediums in the physical world. Of course, one can't help but empathize with a father who has suffered the untimely loss of a much-beloved son. But it seems abundantly clear in *Raymond* that Sir Lodge's spiritualistic attempts to reach his departed son have much more a religious than a scientific character. Lodge even notes that it is important to have faith in the process, because if you are skeptical, that impedes your lost loved ones from making contact with you.

Like Lodge's *Raymond,* the books on spiritualism Lewis was reading in his teens tend to require a deliberate suspension of disbelief on the part of the reader. Given the eminence of those involved in the Society for Psychical Research and their seriousness of purpose, the actual results obtained from all their work are rather slight. In their many volumes of published research projects, one finds an uneven collection of tantalizing anecdotes rather than any compelling evidence. As Jack himself noted, the spiritualist researchers never seemed quite able to make their case. There is always something missing, a final proof that is forthcoming but never quite comes forth. Inevitably there seems to be some hovering doubt about second-hand testimony, gullible witnesses or wonder-workers with a history of fraud. Instead of offering solid evidence for a new kind of faith, this body of research asks readers to put faith in new kinds of "evidence."

Perhaps the most thought-provoking of the psychic researchers was Walter Barrett, the author Lewis recommended to Greeves. This volume is a kind of psychic sampler, examining uncanny occurrences as diverse as telepathy, clairvoyance, divining rods, spirit mediums, poltergeists and automatic writing. Barrett is obviously a serious and careful inquirer, and he is keenly aware of the metaphysical implications of his work. In the introduction he notes that if any of these phenomena can be validated through scientific study, "they will reveal a wide and wonderful extension of human faculties, and give us a glimpse of the abysses of human personality, of depths that transcend time and space and outward things, teaching us that nature is not a soulless interaction of atoms, nor life a paltry misery closed in the grave."

The most easily dismissed chapters in Barrett's book are those focusing on prophets for profit—professional psychics, mediums, crystal ball gazers, automatic writers and the like—most of whom sound like mere mountebanks, and for whom "scientific" scrutiny seems mainly an exercise in credulity.

Far more intriguing are the documented accounts from ordinary people who had no connection to, or interest in, occult studies, but whose uncanny experiences are difficult to account for according to naturalistic principles of causation. Barrett tells of a young English woman who saw a waking vision of her husband, an officer in the British army, fall wounded during the Boer War, cry out to his comrade from the dust, take off his wedding ring and ask that it be given to his wife. Her husband survived the battle, and both he and his brother officer confirmed that the incident happened just as she had envisioned it. In numerous other cases compiled by Barrett, people saw loved ones in great trouble or at time of death, many miles away, often confiding detailed descriptions of the scene to their journals or to friends many days before any actual news arrived.

Perhaps the most engaging account in Barrett's book is the case of Reverend C. W. Sanders of northern Alabama, who had dissociation episodes (or "sleeping spells") for twenty-two years from his midtwenties to late forties. Sanders was called "the Sleeping Preacher" because periodically, sometimes in the middle of a sentence, his head would suddenly nod forward or roll back and then a much more articulate and animated personality would appear, preaching silver-tongued sermons, singing original hymns so soulful and melodious that listeners would weep, telling friends and neighbors where to find a lost key or coin, giving word-for-word transcriptions of letters they had not yet received and sometimes passing on news that a loved one had died several days before official word came from another county or state.

When in his trance state, Sanders would answer only to the name "X+Y=Z" and would refer to his other self not as Sanders, but as "My Casket." When he came out of his "sleeping spells," he was exhausted and dazed, often with nearly unendurable headaches. He never remembered anything about the X+Y=Z episodes, even refusing to believe in them until convinced by the sheer crowd of witnesses.

Initially, Sanders tried to keep his spells a secret, fearing they would destroy his ministry. But his X+Y=Z personality seemed universally admired, so eventually Sanders became resigned to these episodes, deciding they were somehow "of the Lord" like St. Paul's thorn in the flesh. After twenty-two years of this, X+Y=Z wrote a farewell epistle to his "Casket" explaining that he would be returning no more, explaining that the headaches came because, in his altered state, "his head was full of windows" and he could see in every direction, not just out of his eyes, the way the sun shines in every direction. X+Y=Z added that one shouldn't doubt when dying people say they can see loved ones or hear the voices of angels, because that is exactly what happens when the husk of one's physical body begins to peel away. That parting letter was Sanders's last episode; a few days later he reported to his wife that for the first time in over twenty years, he remembered having had a dream the previous night.

The story of Reverend Sanders and his alternate personality sounds, on the face of it, like one of those rural "tall tales." But a book published in 1876 documenting his life listed over one hundred living witnesses to his extraordinary powers, along with an endorsement by William James as well as letters of confirmation from six physicians, ten ministers and a former U. S. Supreme Court justice.

Judging from his later books, Lewis seemed to give a certain credence to the idea of an unsought gift of "second sight," but he rejected all manifestations of the programmed paranormal—seances, ouija boards, automatic writing and the like. In *That Hideous Strength* Jane Studdock has a gift of "dreaming realities"—a gift that she didn't seek and wishes she could get rid of. But throughout the novel, her dreams of what's actually going on at the National Institute of Coordinated Experiments are of considerable help to Ransom and his company as they try to do battle with the dark forces at Belbury. In *The Last Battle* King Tirian, tied to a tree by the Calormenes, calls out to Aslan for help and suddenly sees, in a dream or vision, the Seven Friends of Narnia at a dinner table in England, where they in turn see him only as an apparition. As will be discussed later in this chapter, the older Lewis seemed to contrast sharply in his mind those who experience unplanned occurrences of the paranormal with those who seek out occult powers—and often get more than they bargained for.

As Lewis's materialistic "faith" began to wane near the end of his two years with Kirkpatrick, his interest in spiritualism also began to fade. Lewis later felt he was protected from spiritual debauchery by his practical ignorance of magic, by childlike apprehensions and by an abiding instinct that this was not the road to his ultimate Desire. In *Surprised by Joy* Lewis speculated that he might have ended up as a Satanist or a madman if he had encountered someone during those vulnerable years who dabbled in the dark arts. He added, though, that his reading about forbidden rites also conjured up childhood fears about ghosts, and that he sometimes sought reassurance in materialism as a creed which "promises to exclude the bogies." Most important, however, Lewis came to feel that, even if he could have discovered the proper incantations, the secret formulation of circles, pentangles or other mystic symbols so as to call forth a spirit, though it might be extremely interesting—if one's nerves held up—that really had nothing to do with his real spiritual quest. What did apparitions or levitations have to do with the beloved northern vastnesses of his imagination, the luxuriant island kingdoms for which his soul ached? Eventually he would dismiss his adolescent passion for the paranormal as a kind of "spiritual lust" and dismiss the occultic, like the erotic, as a painted impostor of the true Joy.

Jack's declining interest in the occult turned to outright revulsion after a series of encounters during his undergraduate years at Oxford. As he explains in *Surprised by Joy,* he felt that by the time he returned to the university he had been inoculated against the secret arts, having developed "a wholesome antipathy to everything occult" by the time he reached Oxford and began to encounter "Magicians, Spiritualists, and the like." Even when he felt the allure, he recognized it as a temptation. More important, he had learned that "Joy did not point in that direction."

Almost certainly, the magician referred to in the passage above was William Butler Yeats, the great Irish poet who was more than a little enthralled by matters occult. As Richard Ellman has shown in his classic biography, Yeats was almost obsessed with the paranormal but suppressed this element in his poetry for fear it would damage his literary reputation. Raised by a stern, atheistic father, Yeats steeped himself in spiritualism, theosophy, kabbalism and other hermetic studies as an escape from the claustrophobic this-worldliness of his father's philosophy. Diffident as a young man, Yeats dreamed of using secret and ancient knowledge as a means of transforming himself into a powerful sage and wizard.

Lewis met the great Irish writer in Oxford, expecting to get better acquainted with Yeats the poet, but feeling he had encountered instead Yeats the magician. In October 1919, the same month Jack returned to Oxford after the war, Yeats and his wife, Georgie Hyde Lees, rented a house on Broad Street, opposite Balliol College. Georgie was an accomplished automatic writer (one who wrote out spiritualistic visions while in a trance), and the two of them had barely moved in before they left for an extensive lecture tour in America lasting through the following summer. So members of the univerity town became accustomed to hearing of its illustrious new citizens without seeing much of them.

Jack was anxious to meet someone who had already proven himself a writer of the first order. He had been reading Yeats since he was twelve, both the plays and the poems, and he felt no one, living or dead, spoke for Ireland the way Yeats did. He credited his love of Yeats with saving him from the starchy provincialism of so many of his fellow Ulstermen, for he reveled in the lore of Cuchulain or Fergus as much as any southern Irishman ever did.

On March 14, 1921, Jack received a casual note from an American friend, William Force Stead, saying he was going to visit Yeats that evening after supper and asking if Lewis would like to "come along." Lewis did indeed want to go along, both that evening and again a week later. The two meetings filled him with vivid impressions, and he wrote about them in detail to his father, his brother and his friend Arthur Greeves. For both visits, Stead and Lewis were received in a second-floor parlor in the Broad Street house. This required their climbing a long staircase lined with etchings by

William Blake, chiefly his illustrations for *The Book of Job* and *Paradise Lost*. Blake's most famous etching from the first work portrays a gray-bearded man lying on a coffinlike box and looking down with wide, fearful eyes at claw-handed creatures below him who are clutching at his body and trying to wrap him in a chain. From Milton's epic poem, Blake created images of towering flames, fanged serpents and dog-headed dragons. Not surprisingly, Jack seemed a little unnerved before he even reached the upper floor, pronouncing the Blake pictures "wicked" in one letter and "diabolical" in another.

The large second-floor parlor where Stead and Lewis met Yeats and his party featured bright red curtains and two tall candlesticks like those that stand beside a church altar. There were six high-backed antique chairs arranged in a circle by the hearth, with tables along the side walls holding curiously shaped objects, like instruments from an alchemist's workshop.

Not surprisingly, Yeats dominated the gathering, which included his wife and two other visitors besides Lewis and Stead. He was a big, sallow-skinned man in his late fifties with a shock of ruffled gray hair. Even seated, Yeats was physically imposing, both taller and huskier than Jack expected. He had thick spectacles, a pointed nose and a small mouth, giving him the look of a keen-eyed hawk.

Jack was expecting literary discussion, hoping to play a modern-day Boswell recording Yeats's judgments on drama and poetry, but the talk focused instead on magic, the kabbalah, hermetic knowledge and the mystic meaning of the cycles of the moon. At one point Yeats insisted that a well-known skeptic in Oxford had witnessed a table levitate to the ceiling with a person sitting on it, had vomited at the sight and then had covered up the story and banned all further experiments of that sort from his laboratory.

The following week Lewis was again invited to meet with Yeats in his second-floor parlor. This visit began with the kind of literary talk Jack had expected the first time. But then Jack himself brought up the philosopher Henri Bergson, which made Yeats recall that he had first been tutored in magic by Bergson's sister, wife of a famous Rosicrucian, MacGregor Mathers, who was said to have died a magician's death in a psychic duel with another sorcerer.

Lewis came away from these meetings impressed with Yeats's intelligence and mesmerizing speech, but also amused and put off by the séancelike setting and all the talk of magic. To Warren he described Yeats whimsically as a captivating amalgam of poet, wizard, lunatic and "the most eloquent drunk Irishman you know." To his father he observed more critically that it was a pity to meet a poet of first rank, someone who had known the great minds of his generation, who had become so caught up in the "sham romance of flame-coloured curtains and mumbo-jumbo." Though his encounter with Yeats was a memorable one, his lingering impression seems to have been that Yeats's tremendous creative energy was being squandered on credulous and self-indulgent speculation.

Lewis's distaste for spiritualism was reinforced the following year by his acquaintance with the Reverend Frederick Walker Macran (1866-1947), a friend of Mrs. Moore and her brother, Dr. John Askins. In a sparkling satiric sentence worthy of Dickens, Lewis describes Macran, or "Cranny," in *Surprised by Joy* as "an old, dirty, gabbling, tragic Irish parson who had long since lost his faith but retained his living." Though he was a church rector, Cranny, according to Lewis, had years earlier set aside orthodox Christian doctrine in favor of "evidences" for human survival beyond the grave. This obsession was not linked to any desire to find God, or even to be reunited with lost loved ones; it was a simple, almost monomaniacal, will to surmount death.

Even though he was a long way from being a Christian himself,

Jack was put off not only by the stifling egoism of Macran's spiritualistic interests but also by his hypocrisy. On one occasion in the spring of 1922 he confided to his journal that he had confronted "Cranny" about "why people in his position, who didn't believe that Jesus was a God, spent their time in patching up a sinking ship instead of setting to work on a new one." In other words, why did they remain in the church, trying to rationalize and demythologize supernatural doctrines, instead of starting over with some new, more scientifically respectable religion? Macran answered that just as evolution had reached its peak in the human species, which must go on evolving, religious evolution had reached its peak in Christianity, which must also go on evolving. To this explanation, Jack replied sarcastically in his journal, "I wonder if mastodons talk in the same way."

In a similar mood a year earlier, Lewis had criticized an acquaintance of Yeats's, Father Cyril Martindale, as a "mocker" and "an atheistical dog," even while he remained a Jesuit priest and lecturer on religion at Campion Hall in Oxford. Though he was an unbeliever himself, Jack seemed to have a strong internalized sense of integrity during these years, feeling that those who had lost their faith should have the courage of their nonconvictions and resign from the church. In later years, once he had become a Christian, Lewis would observe that the important distinction in the church was "not between high and low but between religion with real supernaturalism and salvationism on the one hand and all watered-down and modernist versions on the other."

If Jack's attraction to the occult was seriously dampened by his actual meetings with "Magicians, Spiritualists, and the like"—those like Yeats and Macran—his interest was utterly extinguished by a harrowing experience he endured in the spring of 1923. He later described the ordeal in *Surprised by Joy* as a time when he spent fourteen days and nights trying to minister to a man in the process of complete mental collapse During that time Jack had to help "hold him while he kicked and wallowed on the floor, screaming out that devils were tearing him and that he was that moment falling down into Hell." Though he recognized that there were probably physical causes for this disorder, Lewis couldn't help but associate his friend's psychic disintegration with a longtime preoccupation with the occult, including spiritualism and theosophy; he resolved that, as for himself, he would henceforth stick to "the beaten track, the approved road."

Though this ordeal sounds traumatic enough as described in *Surprised by Joy,* it is even more unsettling to read about in the journal Jack kept during his twenties. The man whose breakdown Lewis described was Mrs. Moore's brother, Dr. John H. Askins, who was wounded in World War I and seems never to have fully recovered, either physically or emotionally. Askins, whom Jack familiarly called "the Doc," became a psychoanalyst after the war and developed an intense interest in spiritualism and the possibility of contacting the dead. At first Jack was merely skeptical of these pursuits, asking why ghosts always sounded like they came from the lower middle classes, and commenting that the beliefs of the Doc and his fellow occultists were as much a "ready-made orthodoxy to them as the Bible and Prayer Book are to old fashioned people." But in the winter of 1922-1923, Askins's preoccupation took on increasingly sinister shades. In November he spoke of death and other horrors hanging over everyone and concluded that "if you stopped to think, you wouldn't endure this world for an hour." The following January Jack noted that Doc seemed to have lost interest in every subject except theosophy, and that he had taken to muttering and talking to himself in the bathroom. The next month he started to talk of the "Satanic badness" in the awful depths of one's mind, and he began to look physically wretched, with sunken eyes.

The final breakdown began in earnest in the last week of February, and Jack's journal for the following fortnight describes Askins's screams, grimaces and contortions, spitting fits and paralysis, his flinging himself on the floor and having to be restrained, and his ravings about wrestling with devils. In March Dr. Askins was removed to a medical facility, and in April word came that he had died of heart failure at the age of forty-six.

For those acquainted with the literature of what is sometimes called "possession disorder," Dr. Askins's symptoms, as recorded in Jack's diary, sound very similar to those endured by the young women considered bewitched in Salem in 1692 and by the victims described in Aldous Huxley's *The Devils of Loudun* (1948). Though Jack was unclear about the cause of the breakdown, variously attributed to neurosis, hysteria, "war neurasthenia" or possibly venereal disease, he was emphatically clear about the lessons to be learned. After it was all over he wrote to Arthur Greeves that they were both candidates for neuroses since they had been afraid of their fathers as children, but that it could be avoided. In what is clearly self-directed exhortation, Jack offered this advice to Arthur:

> Keep clear of introspection, of brooding, of spiritualism, of everything eccentric. Keep to work and sanity and open air—to the cheerful & the matter of fact side of things. . . . Above all beware of excessive day dreaming, of seeing yourself in the centre of a drama, of self-pity, and, as far as possible, of fears.

As Walter Hooper has aptly observed, "It would be difficult to exaggerate the effect of this experience on Lewis." From 1923 onward, Lewis would associate magic with a particularly sinister kind of escapism and a possible route to diabolism or dementia. In his book-length poem *Dymer* (1926), written before his return to Christianity, Lewis portrays a magician who looks very much like Yeats, trying to convince a young wanderer, Dymer, that he can recapture "Eden fields long lost by man" by drinking an opiate-like elixir. The magician himself, though, has not found the paradise he promises to others. At night he takes out his sorcerer's books, "like the dog returning to its vomit," to view "his strange heaven and his stranger hell / His secret lust, his soul's dark citadel." Looking through his tomes of Theomagia, Demonology, Chemic Magic, and the Book of the Dead, he dimly recognizes that he is seeking "spirits in the dust of dead men's error / Buying the joys of dream with dreamland terror." The magician sickens at heart, knowing that the time will come when he will "scream alone . . . and roll upon the floor." Yet he still tries to tempt Dymer to join him in his sorcerer's orgy, and when the young man tries to escape, he wounds him with a rifle shot.

Though *Dymer* is an obscure and artistically undistinguished poem, it gives powerful evidence of how far Lewis had moved since his first year at Oxford. In the spring of 1917 Jack was recommending books on psychic research to Arthur and boasting that he had handled a three- hundred-year-old book of spells compiled by the "great magician" Cornelius Agrippa, the sixteenth-century necromancer. Six years later he would consider such works almost literally diabolical.

This change of attitude was permanent, as can be seen in Lewis's later prose fiction. In Shakespeare, a conjurer boasts he can "call spirits from the vasty deep," but the skeptic replies, "Why, so can I, or so can any man. But will they come when you do call for them?" The problem for Lewis's conjurers is that the spirits *do* come when you call them. In *The Last Battle,* for example, the conspirators against King Tirian make a pretense of believing in the

Calormene god Tash and end up calling forth the real thing, a vulture-headed creature with four arms. "People shouldn't call for demons," comments one of the loyal dwarves, "unless they really mean what they say."

In *Perelandra* Lewis presents an even more chilling portrait of one whose dabbling turns to deviltry. When the insidious visionary Edward Weston lectures Elwin Ransom about the emerging cosmic Life Force, grandiosely proclaiming, "I call that Force into me completely," he inadvertently invokes a spirit from hell, and he ends up "rolling at Ransom's feet, slavering and chattering and tearing up moss by the handfuls." From that time onward he is little more than a corpse animated by a demon.

Readers of *Perelandra* have wondered where Lewis derived such a disturbing portrait of evil as the "the Un-man," the possessed body of Weston. It seems very likely that some of the details came from Jack's two-week vigil over Doc Askins in his delirious state. When Ransom looks at the Un-man and feels that "often its grimaces achieved a horrible resemblance to people Ransom had known and loved in our own world," we are reminded of Lewis's description of Askins as "a man whom I had dearly loved, and well he deserved that love." Like Askins, Weston's face is contorted, his body convulsed, and he cries out that devils are trying to take him. When the Un-man tries to tempt the unfallen Eve of that planet by encouraging her to "seize a grand role in the drama of her world," it calls to mind Jack's warning to Arthur about not trying to see himself as the center of the drama. Weston also comments that spiritualism contains more truths than people realize, but that they are hideous truths, recalling the young Lewis's conviction that Doc's fascination for spiritualism had hastened his emotional collapse.

In Lewis's fiction the practice of magic is not always downright diabolical, but it always betokens a cankered soul. Even a "good" wizard like Merlin in *That Hideous Strength* is said to be a soul in need of saving and someone who has become withered by "laying his mind open to something that broadens the environment just a bit too much." For Lewis, the sin of magicians is not just that they dabble in forbidden arts; more seriously, they have succumbed to the serpent's oldest temptation, "Ye shall be as gods."

Magic and *magician* are two more specialized terms in the Lewis lexicon, both in his fiction and his nonfiction. Andrew Ketterley in *The Magician's Nephew* is typical, one who wants to manipulate occult forces for his own gain; who feels exempt from ordinary morality because of his "high and lonely destiny"; who disregards the sanctity of life, whether human or animal. Though he is essentially a comic character, Andrew's "magic" shares a great deal with a misguided sort of scientism Lewis found all too prevalent in the modern era.

In *The Abolition of Man* Lewis warns that, beyond the obvious practical benefits of modern scientific advance, there may emerge a kind of religious energy very much like the old occult arts:

> There is something which unites magic and applied science while separating both from the "wisdom" of earlier ages. For the wise men of old, the cardinal problem had been how to conform the soul to reality, and the solution had been knowledge, self-discipline and virtue. For magic and applied science alike the problem is how to subdue reality to the wishes of men.

Here Lewis touches on one of the themes that was closest to his heart after he had returned to Christianity: learning to accept what is given and to conform one's will to reality, rather than insisting on one's own way and trying to bend reality to one's will. Apart from the intrinsic dangers of the occult, the practice of magic also suggests an underlying attitude of not accepting one's creatureliness, of trying to escape the intractable vulnerability of being human. Lewis expresses this thought most succinctly in "The Inner Ring," where he observes, "It is the very mark of a perverse desire that it seeks what is not to be had."

After his return to faith, Lewis would note in the preface to *The Screwtape Letters* that one can err in both directions, either by discounting the possibility of evil forces outside of humanity or by believing in them and becoming obsessed with the subject. Lewis concludes that fallen spirits "are equally pleased by both errors and hail a materialist and a magician with the same delight."

Between his midteens and his midtwenties Lewis came full circle on this issue. Though he seriously considered both materialism and spiritualism during his Great Bookham years—however illogically—he had emphatically rejected both of these views after his first few years at Oxford. Having explored materialism, mind-matter dualism and spiritualism, Lewis began to explore philosophic Idealism in his quest to understand the underlying relations of matter and spirit. He would later conclude that Idealism was not his final destination but a step in the right direction.

SEVEN

IDEALISM & PANTHEISM
IN THE TWENTIES

In his preface to *The Pilgrim's Regress* Lewis outlines his spiritual journey in one sentence: "On the intellectual side my own progress had been from 'popular realism' to Philosophical Idealism; from Idealism to Pantheism; from Pantheism to Theism; and from Theism to Christianity." By "popular realism" he means his boyhood conviction that the observable world experienced through the senses is the only reality. By his own account, then, neither the mind-matter dualism of the war years nor his interest in spiritualism marked any real advance over the materialism of his adolescence. It was not until he began formal study of philosophy at Oxford that he seemed to take a discernible step forward in his spiritual understanding. In Lewis's summary, it is also important to note the qualifier "on the intellectual side," showing his vivid awareness that philosophical inquiry alone does not make up the whole of one's spiritual journey.

When Lewis returned to University College after the war, he resumed his study in classics and philosophy, taking a First Class Degree in "Mods" (Honour Moderations, Greek and Latin texts) in 1920, and another First in "Greats" (classical history, culture and philosophy) in 1922. Since fellowships in classics and philosophy were extremely scarce during those years, even for someone with his brilliant record, Jack stayed at Oxford another year to study English language and literature, earning yet another First in 1923.

Some students of Lewis have compared a First Class Degree at Oxford to earning an A in a college course in America. But it is more comparable to graduating *summa cum laude* from Harvard or Yale. The examinations in Greats, for example, covered a minimum of two years' worth of lecture and tutorial material. Students wishing to earn a degree in Greats were required to complete two three-hour essay exams on six consecutive days, covering Greek and Roman history, moral and political philosophy, particular topics on Plato, Aristotle and other major figures, as well as translating into English Greek texts not seen before and translating English texts into proper classical Latin. Not surprisingly, those who were awarded "Firsts" on these exams had their names published in newspapers throughout Britain, and the distinction would become a permanent part of their resumé.

Even though Lewis was one of only a handful of people ever to earn three Firsts at Oxford, he was still without a full-time fellowship after completing his undergraduate studies. In the academic year 1924-1925 he accepted a one-year appointment as a lecturer and tutor in philosophy at University College, filling in for one of his own tutors who was lecturing in America. This position afforded Jack the opportunity for broad and careful reading in philosophy, from the ancients, whom he already knew well in the original Greek and Latin, to the moderns, including living contemporaries such as Bertrand Russell and Henri Bergson.

During this time Lewis embraced Idealism, the philosophy that the world of the senses is but an appearance, that the ultimate reality is a trans-empirical Absolute, "the fuller splendor behind the sensuous curtain." Jack had first encountered Idealism during his brief stint at Oxford before the Great War. In July 1917 Lewis wrote to Arthur Greeves about his budding interest in philosophy, saying he was busy reading George Berkeley's *Principles of Human Knowledge* (1710). Lewis reported that in the section he had just finished, Bishop Berkeley was writing "to prove the existence of God—which he does by disproving the existence of matter." Despite this whimsical summary, Jack was interested in Berkeley's metaphysics, called subjective idealism, and suggested to Greeves that the two of them read the whole book together and correspond about it.

Berkeley argues that the material things we see around us are actually objects in the mind of God, and that consciousness, not matter, is the ultimate reality. His famous dictum was *Esse es percipi,* "To be is to be perceived." This premise may have logical merits, but it is highly counterintuitive, since it contradicts all the evidence of the senses about what constitutes the real world. It is not surprising that Berkeley should become a figure of fun among those at Oxford studying philosophy. The common critique was waggishly expressed as a limerick:

> There was a young man who said, "God
> Must think it exceedingly odd
> If he finds that this tree
> Continues to be
> When there's no one about in the Quad."

To this an apparent Berkeley supporter penned a limerick in reply:

Dear Sir: Your astonishment's odd:
I am always about in the Quad,
And that's why the tree
Will continue to be,
Since observed by
                              Yours faithfully,
                              God

Berkeley's contention that the material universe was actually an idea in the mind of God seems to have been a bit too exotic for the young Lewis, for we hear no more of the bishop in his books or letters. Another Idealist whom Lewis read early on, and set aside early on, was the French philosopher Henri Bergson. Though he always remembered Bergson's critique of Schopenhauer's nihilistic philosophy, Lewis was not attracted to Bergson's own views, his idea of an *élan vital,* or Life Force, pressing forward from lower species to higher and from higher species to whatever else the future might bring.

At first Lewis simply found this philosophy, set forth in Bergson's *Creative Evolution* (1907), difficult to grasp in concrete terms. Later he came to see it as a dangerous deification of Spirit itself, missing the crucial obligation to discern among spirits. In *Perelandra,* for example, when the monomaniacal Weston offers his paean to the Life Force, a philosophy referred to as "Creative Evolution" in the text, Ransom the Christian answers warily, "One wants to be careful about this sort of thing. There are spirits and spirits you know." At the cost of his own soul, Weston learns too late the truth of Ransom's warning. (Interestingly, Bergson himself continued to evolve in his thinking about the Life Force. Though he would be forever famous as the philosopher of the *élan vital,* Bergson took an increasing interest in Christianity in later years and was baptized into the Roman Catholic Church shortly before his death in 1941.)

After these early encounters with theistic idealism and evolutionary idealism, Lewis became increasingly attracted to another school of Idealists, the "English Hegelians." These included T. H. Green (1836-1882), F. H. Bradley (1846-1924) and Bernard Bosanquet (1848-1923), all theorists whom he read in depth when he began studying and teaching philosophy in the twenties.

Lewis calls Green, Bradley and Bosanquet "mighty names" in the twenties and refers to these three again in the preface to *The Pilgrim's Regress* as the "dynasty" that most shaped his own brand of Idealism. As their name implies, all three took as their point of departure Friedrich Hegel's idea that world history is the process of a transcendent Reason unfolding itself in the material world and in human minds. This is clearly a metaphysical notion, and it goes without saying that the British Idealists were fierce opponents of materialism and of the new empiricism which was becoming so influential in the natural sciences.

T. H. Green, in his *Prolegomena to Ethics* (1883), argued that the human mind has an empirical aspect, the brain function of the physical organism, and a metaphysical aspect, which is "the vehicle of an eternally complete consciousness." In this view God is not a person but an "infinite subject" gradually becoming incorporated into finite human minds. Lay readers who find such a concept difficult to grasp may take comfort that trained philosophers feel much the same way. Frederick Copleston, in his *History of Philosophy,* comments that Green's writings too often lapse into the kind of "vague and woolly speculation which has done so much to bring metaphysical idealism into disrepute."

Despite his euphonious name, Bernard Bosanquet has, like Green, become little more than a footnote in the history of philosophy. Bosanquet applied Hegelianism to political philosophy, arguing that just as the Absolute is composed of all conscious individuals, the political state is a concrete embodiment of the "General Will" of individuals in that country. After the carnage of World War I, it was clear to everyone that actions of the principal states involved did *not* reflect the general will of the people, and Bosanquet's political philosophy declined in influence as rapidly as his metaphysics.

F. H. Bradley's influence lasted somewhat longer, both on philosophy in general and on Lewis in particular. (Bradley was also an inspiration to the young T. S. Eliot, who wrote his doctoral dissertation about Bradley's Idealism and its implications for literature.) Bradley was the son of a stern evangelical preacher, and though he set aside his father's religious beliefs, he retained a conviction that one's worldview must be grounded in metaphysical realities. Bradley scorned nineteenth-century empiricism and utilitarianism as mechanistic ethical systems ungrounded in first principles.

In his most influential book, *Appearance and Reality* (1893), Bradley envisioned an all-embracing Absolute in which the contradictions and illusions of the sensory world are transcended and resolved. This Absolute should not be confused with the God of religion, because it is not a Person apart from the universe; rather it is immanent in the universe, transforming the physical into the metaphysical. Just as each human body has a "soul," the Absolute is the "soul" of the cosmos. For critics who wondered how Bradley could seem to know so much about an "unknowable" Absolute or how it could seem both personal and transpersonal, Bradley tended to accept the contradictions, arguing that flawed human logic cannot penetrate that which transcends both reason and imagination. For a professional philosopher he was surprisingly skeptical about the efficacy of human reasoning. In a famous aphorism he observed that "metaphysics is the finding of bad reasons for what we believe on instinct, but to find these reasons is no less an instinct."

Commentators on Bradley have noted the similarity of his thought to the basic tenets of Hinduism, the idea that the atman, individual soul, of all living things comprise the Brahma, or Universal Soul. This "Oversoul" cannot be known directly because the physical world is Maya, a veil of deceptive appearances. When Lewis declared in "De Futilitate" that the "only two serious philosophical options for an adult mind" are Hinduism and Christianity, he was probably thinking not of the complex religious traditions of India, which he had not studied in any depth, but of this Eastern religion's broad outlines as enunciated in the philosophy of F. H. Bradley. Though Bradley is usually classified as an Idealist, Lewis calls this philosophy pantheism because of its assertion that the Absolute is immanent in nature, not above it.

Nowadays pantheism is considered by many to be a New Age religion, and catch phrases such as "the Force be with you" make it seem almost like the space-age religion of the future. But as Lewis reminds us in *Miracles,* pantheism is actually an age-old religion, found in aboriginal societies around the world, in pre-Socratic Greece and in India since time immemorial. He concludes that, "far from being the final religious refinement, Pantheism is in fact the permanent natural bent of the human mind." After all, since humans are both body and spirit (the inner world of consciousness), why should not animals, and even plants, have spirits of their own? And why should not the whole cosmos itself have a Universal Soul?

For most of his twenties Lewis considered varieties of Idealism, first in the hazy formulations of Green and Bosanquet, then in the more specific, and more pantheistic, version presented by Bradley. But the hallmark of Lewis's mind throughout his life was clarity, and he couldn't help but question the logical consistency of the Idealists. It bothered him even more that they did not seem especially concerned about the issue of coherence. As he saw the problem, the more befuddled and contradictory their arguments became, the more they fell back on the notion that human reasoning is confined to the world of Appearance and cannot access Reality. But if discursive thought is so impotent to discover bedrock reality, then why should we believe the Idealists' model of the Absolute over anyone else's? And couldn't any religious system, no matter how nonsensical, hide its intellectual shoddiness behind the claim that finite human reason cannot grasp transcendent mysteries?

Lewis was also bothered by the unacknowledged borrowing of the Idealists and their predecessors. While presenting their ideas as the latest advance in philosophy and the product of uncompromising analysis, they were actually heavily dependent on earlier thinkers and age-old religious traditions. In *The Pilgrim's Regress* young John the seeker is quite impressed by the Idealists until he comes across them at night "raiding the pantry," drawing their intellectual sustenance and emotional appeal from traditional religions and philosophies, including Judaism, Christianity and even theosophy.

Lewis's incisive mind seemed to insist on a clearer conception of the Absolute. It was this quest for clarity that moved him from a vaguely defined Absolute which was simply assumed to exist (Idealism) to one defined as immanent in the universe, the "soul" of the cosmos (pantheism)—and then to an Absolute which is somehow apart from and above the physical realm (theism). All his reading in the ethical philosophy of the ancients had trained him to link Truth and Goodness, to feel that one's metaphysics should undergird one's morals. It bothered him that pantheism had no "cost of discipleship" whatsoever, that it seemed merely an idea without any ideals. As he later explained in *Miracles,* "The Pantheist's God does nothing, demands nothing. He is there if you wish for Him, like a book on a shelf. He will not pursue you." In the same passage Lewis goes on to contrast the "tame" God of Idealism and pantheism with the God of Christian faith:

> An impersonal God—well and good. A subjective God of beauty, truth and goodness, inside our own heads—better still. A formless life-force surging through us, a vast power which we can tap—best of all. But God Himself, alive, pulling at the other end of the cord, perhaps approaching at an infinite speed, the hunter, king, husband—that is quite another matter. . . . There comes a moment when people who have been dabbling in religion ("Man's search for God"!) suddenly draw back. Supposing we really found Him? We never meant it to come to *that!* Worse still, supposing He had found us?

This, of course, is exactly what happened to Lewis himself, as he entered his midtwenties. He describes the process rather obscurely in *The Pilgrim's Regress,* but the running titles to the pages tell all we need to know about this phase of his journey: "As soon as he attempts seriously to live by Philosophy, it turns into Religion" and "From Pantheism to Theism. The transcendental I becomes *Thou.*"

With pantheism, as with eroticism and occultism in earlier years, there came the old question, But what about Joy? What does this have to do with the inconsolable longing? This time, though, there was a genuine advance. Whereas former pursuits had led to false objects of Joy, Lewis felt this new approach was more fruitful. It assumed a genuine Absolute, something beyond the finite world where all human questions disappeared, where paradoxes were resolved. The Idealist's concept of the Absolute, he concludes, "had much of the quality of Heaven." Unfortunately, this was a heaven one could never know, since it was, by definition, eternally out of reach for those in the finite realm. Yet Lewis the pilgrim was making some progress: the "great glory" he used to associate with Northern myths, which he did not believe in, could now be admired in the Absolute, something he did believe in.

Apart from feeling that he had at least glimpsed the true object of Joy, Lewis at this time also came to redefine Joy itself. In the spring of 1924 Jack first read Samuel Alexander's *Space, Time and Deity* and wrote in his diary that he was "greatly impressed by the author's truthful antithesis of enjoyment and contemplation." Though his terminology is peculiar, Alexander makes a useful distinction between experiencing something directly and unself-consciously ("enjoyment") versus thinking about the experience, watching oneself have the experience ("contemplation"). If something makes you glad (or mad or sad), you are "enjoying" the moment directly; but if you stop and observe your own emotion at that time, you are "contemplating," observing your own inner states of mind. Alexander comments that the two mental processes may alternate rapidly but cannot take place simultaneously. One cannot be both unself-conscious and self-conscious at the same time.

This distinction was extremely useful for Lewis, helping him resolve a problem that had bothered him since childhood. As with many persons with acute sensibilities, Lewis sometimes suffered from an excessive self-consciousness in which he seemed to observe himself in the very moment of acting, thinking or feeling. One of the reasons he set aside his childhood faith was that he developed the habit of watching himself in the act of prayer, trying to gauge his own sincerity even as he uttered the words. Of course, the very act of watching oneself undermines one's sense of sincerity.

In his early twenties Jack had discussed this tendency toward double-mindedness with Mrs. Moore's brother, Doc Askins, who diagnosed it as a mild form of dissociation. But the Doc's mental collapse and death soon afterward confirmed Lewis's distrust of psychoanalytic approaches to self-understanding. He grew increasingly to distrust introspection and "motive-scratching" as an invitation to narcissism and self-absorption. Repeatedly in his later books and letters he advises readers simply to do what they know to be their duty and not to wait for the right motives or the right feelings to present themselves to the mind. As for his own problem with an unblinking inward gaze, he learned to seek respite from the prattler, the self-watcher, in vigorous conversation, in reading and in prayer. He also used writing for this purpose. Though most writers find the composition process to be arduous and mentally taxing, Lewis often wrote in the evenings for relaxation, enjoying the mental focus on his subject, not himself, and also taking pleasure in the physical act of dipping the pen in an inkstand and pulling it across a page.

The distinction between enjoying and contemplating also had important implications for Lewis's understanding of Joy. More and more he came to see that it was not Joy itself, a desirable mental state, he was seeking; rather it was that to which Joy pointed. He realized that those things which evoked Joy—Asgard in Norse myth, or Hesperides in Greek myth—were not its true object, but only reminders of a deeper reality.

If by his midtwenties Lewis began to think that the Absolute might be personal, he came increasingly to wonder in his late twenties if this Person might be the God in whom Christians believed. He was attracted by the writings of G. K. Chesterton, especially *The Everlasting Man,* which he first read in 1926, the year after it was published. He enjoyed Chesterton not only for his robust humor but also for a sense of sincere goodness evident in his books. Finding an unexpected cogency in Chesterton's outline of history, Lewis began to feel that "Christianity itself was very sensible 'apart from its Christianity.' " This paradox was deepened when Lewis began to realize that most of the authors he found intellectually nourishing (Spenser, Milton, Johnson and MacDonald, among others) took seriously "Christian mythology," while those who "did not suffer from religion" (Voltaire, Gibbon, Mill, Wells, Shaw) seemed thin and "tinny" by comparison. More and more it seemed to him that the profound writers were profoundly deluded by their faith, but the clear-seeing unbelievers did not see very far.

Moreover, several of the men at Oxford to whom Lewis was most attracted were also practicing Christians. First he met Neville Coghill, clearly intelligent, well-informed, but also a Christian and "a thoroughgoing supernaturalist." Later, when Lewis became a fellow at Magdalen College, he got to know J. R. R. Tolkien and Hugo Dyson, two more kindred spirits who turned out to be Christians.

Increasingly, Lewis's problem of belief came to be linked with his old dilemma about intellect and imagination, dating back at least as far as his writing of "The Quest of Bleheris." As late as 1927, ten years after he had arrived at Oxford, Lewis recorded in a diary his personal restiveness and philosophical turmoil, clearly linking the two issues: "[Today I] was thinking about imagination and intellect and the unholy muddle I am in about them at present: undigested scraps of anthroposophy and psychoanalysis jostling with orthodox idealism over a background of good old Kirkian rationalism. Lord, what a mess! And all the time (with me) there's the danger of falling back into most childish superstitions, or of running into dogmatic materialism to escape them."

This "mess" began to sort itself out when Lewis was thirty. He seemed to have had an almost mystical experience in the summer of 1929 while riding on a bus in Oxford. Without words or clear mental pictures, he became aware that he was "holding something at bay, or shutting something out." He felt he was being presented with a free choice, that of opening a door or letting it stay shut. He said he felt no weight of compulsion or duty, no threats or rewards, only a vivid sense that "to open the door . . . meant the incalculable."

Of course, his instinct was to play it safe, to avoid walking through the door. As he explains, his great desire had always been to "call his soul his own," to avoid interference. Yet here was a call for total surrender, an overwhelming sense that it was time to relinquish all.

Perhaps it is because of this vivid experience that we find so often in Lewis's fiction the door as a symbol of giving up one's freedom, allowing oneself to be drawn in and to make a commitment. In *Perelandra* the narrator, "Lewis," explains his anxiety on approaching Ransom's isolated cottage: "I suppose everyone knows this fear of getting 'drawn in'—the moment at which a man realises that what had seemed to him mere speculations are on the point of landing him in the Communist Party or the Christian Church— the sense that a door has just slammed and left him on the inside."

In *That Hideous Strength* it is Jane Studdock who will "not get mixed up in it, would not be drawn in," who considers it one of the first principles of her life "to avoid entanglements and interferences." Yet, willy nilly she is drawn into the conflict and uses her clairvoyance to help Ransom, now the Pendragon, stay apprised of what is happening among the enemy. But as Ransom says, "Our Lord does all things for each," and she has been brought to St. Anne's not only for what she can offer but also for what she can receive: in the course of the novel she undergoes a complete spiritual transformation. She had associated Religion with "the smell of pews, . . . horrible confirmation classes, the nervous affability of clergymen." But she comes to sense that there are "alarming and operative realities" in the spiritual realm, that there might actually be a God, as well as life after death, heaven and hell. She came to St. Anne's with her own vague pantheistic notions of Religion, something about "a kind of exhalation or a cloud of incense, something steaming up from specially gifted souls toward a receptive heaven." But at St. Anne's they didn't talk about Religion but about God: "They had no picture in their minds of some mist steaming upward: rather of strong, skilful hands thrust down to make, and mend, perhaps even to destroy."

Jane's actual moment of conversion conveys vividly what Lewis himself must have been feeling in the summer of 1929:

> A boundary had been crossed. She had come into a world, or into a Person, or into the presence of a Person. Something expectant, patient, inexorable, met her with no veil or protection between. . . . In this height and depth and breadth the little idea of herself which she had hitherto called *me* dropped down and vanished, unfluttering, into bottomless distance, like a bird in a space without air. The name *me* was the name of a being whose existence she had never suspected, a being which did not yet fully exist, but which was demanded. It was a person (not the person she had thought), yet also a thing, a made thing, made to please Another and in Him to please all others. . . . And the making went on amidst a kind of splendour or sorrow or both, whereof she could not tell whether it was in the moulding hands or in the kneaded lump.

In the end Jane's world is remade, and she herself is remade. Her first act of obedience is to try to reconstruct her shattered marriage with Mark Studdock, who has narrowly escaped spiritual destruction after being recruited by the conspirators at the National

Institute of Coordinated Experiments. In the last scene of the novel she goes to the lodge where her husband is staying but hesitates before opening the latch and going through the door. Barraged by doubts, she nonetheless summons up her courage and resolves that "it was high time that she went in."

In the summer of 1929, not long after his experience on the bus, Lewis himself decided that it was high time he went in. In *Surprised by Joy* he offers this simple explanation of that dramatic moment: "In the Trinity Term of 1929 I gave in, and admitted that God was God, and knelt and prayed: perhaps, that night, the most dejected and reluctant convert in all England."

EIGHT

FINDING TRUTH
IN THE OLD BELIEFS

Lewis's testimony has confused some readers, for he seems to record two conversion experiences, one in 1929 and another in 1931. In *Surprised by Joy* Lewis writes about himself as a dejected and reluctant convert kneeling and praying in the summer of 1929. But then he quickly adds that this was only a conversion to "Theism, pure and simple, not to Christianity." He goes on explain that he began attending his parish church on Sundays and college chapels not because he believed in Christianity but because he thought he ought to make some overt gesture about where his sympathies lay.

It would have been easy for Lewis to tidy up his recollections a bit and choose one dramatic moment in which he reclaimed his childhood faith. But he wanted to record his progress with all possible accuracy, and it is obvious he felt that the process only began in 1929 and was not completed until 1931. His distinction between "Theism" and "Christianity" is not entirely satisfactory, for it is clear that he was surrendering the first time to a Person visualized as the God of the Bible, not of the Koran or the kabbalah. Yet his letters to Arthur Greeves during that two-year period do indeed reveal that his conversion came on steadily, not suddenly. Owen Barfield has said that the word *conversion* itself is not quite accurate to describe Lewis's spiritual development in this period, since it usually connotes sudden, radical transformation.

It is important to note that Lewis depicts himself as a "dejected and reluctant convert" the first time around, almost as if his mind were taking him where his heart did not want to go. The distinction between the two conversions might be best interpreted in terms of the medieval model of human personality, which Lewis explains in *The Screwtape Letters*. In this view the inner self can be envisioned as three concentric circles, with one's will at the center, intellect in the second circle and imagination in the outer circle. First an idea or image enters into the mind's eye, then one grasps it intellectually and finally one acts on it. Lewis's long, drawn-out conversion process illustrates the model perfectly. His imagination was baptized back in 1916, when he first read MacDonald and was entranced by "the beauty of holiness." His intellect had shown him by 1929 that the Absolute must indeed be God, but it was not until 1931 that he recognized the claims of Christ and surrendered his will.

Lewis recalls that his father's death in September 1929 had no direct bearing on his recovery of faith. This seems accurate enough since the process had already begun earlier that summer. Yet this period of spiritual healing was almost certainly reinforced and deepened by the emotional healing that occurred in the last month of Albert Lewis's life.

The low point of the relationship between father and son had come ten years earlier, when Jack was twenty, during a time when the two brothers were visiting their father on summer holiday in 1919. Albert found some unpaid bills Jack had tried to hide from him and irritably confronted his son with the evidence. The younger Lewis, resenting this interference into his personal affairs, responded fiercely, complaining that he had lost respect and confidence in his father, dredging up incidents going all the way back to childhood. According to his diary, Albert Lewis expected an apology for this tirade, but his son never offered one. That fall Jack set up a joint household with Mrs. Moore and her daughter Maureen in Oxford, and bitter feelings between him and his father lasted for several months.

Gradually the two of them put the incident behind them, and their relationship seems to have improved throughout Jack's twenties. When he was awarded the prestigious fellowship at Magdalen, the first thing Jack did was sit down and write a sincere letter of gratitude to Albert for all the years of financial assistance. He thanked his father for six years of generous financial backing, saying that that alone had allowed him to continue his studies while other young men of equal ability had been forced to drop out. He concludes, "You have waited, not only without complaint but full of encouragement, while chance after chance slipped away and when the goal receded furthest from sight. Thank you again and again."

This is certainly one of the most eloquent letters of thanks a son could write to his father, and it may well have expressed feelings that Albert had been hoping to hear for many years. Through all those years of financial support—including quarrels over unpaid bills—it seems that Jack wanted to feel grateful but felt instead a certain resentment at his own dependency and his father's prying into his private life. But once Jack was assured of some measure of monetary self-sufficiency, it seemed to free him to confess frankly his gratitude and affection.

Their relationship continued on this more cordial note through-out Jack's late twenties. Then in August 1929 he received news in Oxford that Albert was seriously ill. He responded promptly, writing a letter even more openly affectionate than the one he had sent on receiving his fellowship, addressing his father as "My dear, dear Papy," saying that he would come to Belfast as soon as possible, and closing, "With all my love and best wishes, your loving son." Jack did cross over the Irish Sea to take care of his father in his last illness, which was diagnosed as colon cancer. Albert was glad to have his son with him and seemed surprisingly cheerful, given his condition. His demanding personality was still in evidence as he insisted on hearing what Jack was saying in his letters to Warren, and even told his son which stationery and envelopes to use. But there was no question now about interference, about Jack reserving time for himself. He had to surrender to the situation, to be there for his father day or night.

When Albert learned from his doctors that he needed to undergo immediate surgery, Jack wrote to Warren that their father was "taking it like a hero." In these last days Jack underwent a profound reversal of perspective. As A. N. Wilson has observed about this period, "All of a sudden, Jack saw that his father *was* a sort of hero—a maddening, eccentric hero but a man whose decency, courage and good humour were as unshakable as his sincere piety." In those few weeks the elder and younger Lewis found a serenity and closeness in their relationship which they had perhaps not known before.

Albert seemed briefly to rally after the operation, so much so that Jack returned to Oxford to prepare for the fall term. But after only two days, Jack was called back to Belfast, arriving on September 25 to learn that his father had died the previous day, at the age of sixty-six.

Both Jack and Warren considered their father an enduring fixture in their lives, and neither seemed prepared for the loss. In October Jack wrote to his brother at an army post in Shanghai that he had always considered it sentimental and hypocritical for people to think and speak differently of a person once that person had died. But now he saw that it was a natural process. In the last days, he said, he had felt "mere pity for the poor old chap and for the life he had led." Then he explained his lingering feelings: "As time goes on, the thing that emerges is that, whatever else he was, he was a terrific *personality*. . . . How he filled a room. How hard it was to realize that physically he was not a big man. Our whole world is either direct or indirect testimony to the same fact. . . . The way we enjoyed going to Little Lea, and the way we hated it, and the way we enjoyed hating it; as you say, one can't grasp that *that* is over."

Having spent so many years fretting over how his father treated him, Jack now had begun to contemplate how he had treated his father. He and his brother had long referred to Albert as "Pudaita" or "the Pudaitabird," after his rounded Irish pronunciation of the word potato. This suggests that part of their condescension toward their father was less personal than social, the attitude of two English-educated schoolboys toward their Irish forebear, whom they considered parochial and unsophisticated. Jack himself was aware of this snobbish element in his feelings toward his father after he had been at Oxford only a short while. Later he also came to recognize that he and Warren had developed a habitually captious attitude toward their father, becoming annoyed with the same eccentricities in him which they considered amusing or endearing in other elderly men. In the long term, Jack became deeply ashamed about this; his father had led a lonely life, had reached out to his sons for companionship, and they had spurned him. The summer after his father's death Jack wrote to Arthur that he realized he had treated his father "abominably." In 1954, the year he was composing *Surprised by Joy,* Lewis wrote to a friend that no sin in his own life was worse than his insensitive treatment of his father.

For both brothers, the death of their father also called to mind their mother's passing twenty-one years earlier. Warren confessed to his diary that he was glad to have been in China in those final weeks, for he didn't think he could have endured another parting like the earlier one. With the settling of Albert Lewis's estate, Warren also inherited a great mass of diaries, letters and papers from both the Lewis and Hamilton sides of the family. He spent several years arranging, editing and typing these papers, ending up with over thirty-five hundred pages of material, arranged in eleven volumes, which he called *Memoirs of the Lewis Family, 1850-1930.*

One of the most significant items Warren discovered in this mountain of papers was his father's diary, in which the latter had recorded his wife's conversation on her deathbed. Albert wrote that Flora had advised her sickroom nurse that, when it came time to marry, she should find "a good man who loves you and who loves God." They had been quietly discussing the goodness of God when Flora asked suddenly, "What have we done for Him?" To this quotation, Albert had added, "May I never forget that."

It would be difficult for either of her sons to forget that either. Jack, as well as Warren, was sifting through the family papers during this time, and one cannot help but feel that both were deeply affected. Lewis had associated his father's faith with the "political churchgoing of Ulster" and with his own youthful hypocrisy in pretending to believe, even taking Communion, just to avoid a row. But here was a reminder that their dear, lost mother—cheerful, tranquil, daughter of gentlefolk—had also been an earnest

Christian. Surely she would want the same thing for her sons that she wanted for her nurse's future husband. It is interesting to note that in *The Pilgrim's Regress,* once John has symbolically recovered his faith and returned to his homeland, he comes upon his parents' old homestead and begins to weep: "We have come back to Puritania," he said, "and that was my father's house. I see that my father and mother are gone already beyond the brook. I had much I would have said to them."

The process that was begun in 1929 with Jack's conversion to theism continued, sometimes fitfully, for the next two years. His letters during that period make it clear that he was on the move spiritually but that he hadn't yet reached his destination. In December 1929 Jack confessed to Arthur that he had found and was still "finding more and more, the element of truth in the old beliefs." Over the Christmas holiday he and Warren attended church services together, and in January 1930 Jack wrote three letters to Arthur Greeves reporting on his spiritual condition. On January 9 the critic seemed to hold sway, as he told Arthur that despite his recent change of perspective, the popular view of Christ derived from the Gospels could be obtained only by "picking & choosing & slurring over a good deal." On January 26 Jack wrote on a more positive note that he had finished reading George MacDonald's *Diary of an Old Soul* and was looking for other books of that kind, adding, "That is another of the beauties of coming, I won't say, to religion but to an attempt at religion—one finds oneself on the main road with all humanity, and can compare notes with an endless succession of previous travellers. It is emphatically coming home."

Only four days later he wrote again, saying that things were continuing to go well for him spiritually, though he tried not to take pride in his progress, knowing that it came from the grace of

God, not from his own efforts. He goes on to offer a perceptive self-diagnosis, saying that his spiritual life is still hampered by pride and a deep-seated desire to call his soul his own: "There seems to be no end to it. Depth under depth of self-love and self-admiration. Closely connected with this is the difficulty I find in making even the faintest approach to giving up my own will: which as everyone has told us is the only thing to do."

The next month he wrote to Owen Barfield in a tone of humorous panic: "Terrible things are happening to me. The 'Spirit' or 'Real I' is showing an alarming tendency to become much more personal and is taking the offensive, and behaving just like God. You'd better come on Monday at the latest or I may have entered a monastery." During the next year, one finds few references to Lewis's spiritual state as explicit as this one, though he often wrote to others about his reading of Dante and George MacDonald, and he told Arthur Greeves that he had begun writing religious poetry of his own.

Then on October 1, 1931, came the definitive word, as Jack wrote to Arthur, "I have just passed on from believing in God to definitely believing in Christ—in Christianity," adding that his "long night talk with Dyson and Tolkien had a good deal to do with it."

Jack had described his long night talk with J. R. R. Tolkien and Hugo Dyson in a letter to Arthur the previous week, saying that the three of them had begun talking about metaphor and myth just after dinner, had continued the conversation as they strolled along Addison's Walk near Jack's rooms at Magdalen College and that he had not gotten to bed until four in the morning. This conversation might well be considered the defining moment in Jack's life, for it helped him resolve issues he had been grappling with since boyhood. In particular, it gave him a way to understand the incarnation as the historical fulfillment of Dying God myths found in many cultures.

Tolkien and Dyson, who shared Lewis's reverence for myth, romance and fairy tale, showed him that mythology reveals its own kind of truth and that Christianity is true mythology. Lewis had insisted that myths were nothing more than "lies breathed through silver," but Tolkien and Dyson answered that myth was better understood as "a real though unfocused gleam of divine truth falling on human imagination." They argued that one of the great and universal myths, that of the dying God who sacrifices himself for the people, shows an innate awareness of the need for redemption not by one's own works, but as a gift from some higher realm. For them, the incarnation was the pivotal point at which myth became history. The life, death and resurrection of Christ not only fulfilled Old Testament types but also embodied—literally—central motifs found in all the world's mythologies.

Ironically, their arguments had been anticipated five years earlier in the unlikeliest of sources. In *Surprised by Joy* Lewis reports that in 1926 a fellow don whom he considered a hard-boiled atheist commented that the evidence for the historicity of the Gospels was surprisingly good. "Rum thing," the skeptic had concluded. "All that stuff of Frazer's about the Dying God. Rum thing. It almost looks as if it had really happened once." From Lewis's diary we know that this hard-boiled atheist was T. D. Weldon (1896-1958), who resembles a great deal the flashy and immoral Dick Devine of the Ransom trilogy. In his diary Lewis wrote that Weldon was "determined to be a villain" and that he "believes he has seen through everything and lives at rock bottom." Yet in his entry for April 26, 1926, Lewis records Weldon's opinion that there was a lot about the historicity of the Gospels that could not be explained away, which would qualify him as a "Christian 'of a sort.' " Coming from a man determined to be a villain (and whom Lewis determined to use as a villain in his later fiction), this remark remained little more than a psychological curiosity at the time. But coming from two of his closest friends, and forcefully argued well into the night, the idea found its mark in 1931, leaving a lasting impression on his imagination, his intellect and finally his will.

Tolkien and Dyson's view of myth offered Lewis a way to justify his lifelong love of mythology and to cross the threshold into the household of Christian faith. No more were his beloved Greek myths, Nordic sagas and Irish legends mere escapist tripe unworthy of a thinking person. They became reservoirs of transrational truths; they provided insights, admittedly partial and distorted, about realities beyond the reach of logical inquiry. In Christianity, the true myth to which all the others were pointing, Lewis found a worldview that he could defend as both *good* and *real*. It was a faith grounded in history and one that satisfied even his formidable intellect.

For Lewis, Christianity would thence become the fountainhead of all myths and tales of enchantment, the key to all mythologies, the myth that unfolded itself in history. About a month after Lewis's conversation with Tolkien and Dyson, he wrote to his brother about a book he had discovered by William Law, an eighteenth-century devotional writer, aptly titled *An Appeal to All That Doubt or Disbelieve*. Unlike all those tentative letters he had been sending to Arthur the past two years, Jack's response clearly shows that he now saw his newfound faith not as "an attempt at religion," but as reality: "[This is] one of those rare works which make you say of Christianity, 'Here is the very thing you like in poetry and the romances, but this time it's true.' "

For Lewis the incarnation became the archetype of a larger pattern, the principle of descent and reascent. In *Miracles* he calls this the "very formula of reality." Plants produce seeds which must fall to the ground and die before new life can begin. Animals and humans produce seeds and eggs which, useless by themselves, form a union at the most elemental level to produce offspring. And the myths of many cultures tell of "corn-kings" who die and rise again for the sake of their people. The incarnation fulfills this mythic pattern, as the King of heaven descends to earth in order to raise it up. Lewis compares the incarnate Christ to a strong man who must stoop low under a heavy burden in order to lift it on his shoulders. Or he is like a diver who must plunge downward into the depths in order to reascend with the precious object he has gone to recover.

This last analogy reveals another important dimension of descent and reascent, the symbolic death and resurrection in Christian baptism. In June 1930, during Lewis's personal two-year *preparatio evangelico,* he wrote to Arthur Greeves that Owen Barfield had taught him how to plunge headfirst into a river, and that he had found an important religious significance in the art of diving. This hint is developed more fully in the climactic scene of *The Pilgrim's Regress,* a chapter titled *Securus Te Projice,* "Throw yourself down safely," a quotation from Augustine. The pilgrim John, stranded in the impassable gorge Peccatum Adae ("Sin of Adam"), awakens one moonlit night and tries to find his way out. He encounters the hideous face of Death itself, who offers the sober reassurance that "the cure of death is dying. He who lays down his liberty in that act receives it back," then tells him to descend to the floor of the canyon. There John meets Mother Kirk (Christianity), her crown and scepter glinting in the bright moonlight, who instructs him that his only escape is to dive into the water, swim downward and emerge on the other side of the mountain. John is full of doubts, pleads that he doesn't know how to dive and feels that the very bitterness of death awaits him. Yet he takes the plunge, learning many mysteries and "dying many deaths," emerging finally in green forests beyond the mountain—along with many other pilgrims whom he hadn't noticed in all his earlier peregrinations. They march westward together until they come upon a beach, and there before him in the morning sun John sees the island that he has been seeking all his life. The next chapter, the beginning of John's regress after his symbolic death and rebirth, is titled after a phrase in Dante's *Paradiso:* "In His will is our peace."

The island in *The Pilgrim's Regress* symbolizes Joy throughout the story, though in the end John learns that it is only a symbol, not his final destination. When Lewis at last became a Christian, he also ended his quest to grasp Joy and resolved the "dialectic of desire" that he had been puzzling over since childhood. If, as Christian doctrine teaches, all humans are exiles from paradise, then how natural that they should feel pangs of longing, painful in their fallenness yet pleasurable in that they point to genuine realities in which they may someday partake. In *Surprised by Joy* Lewis says that once he became a believer again, his intense interest in Sweet Desire receded. He came to feel that it was not really Joy he had been seeking but rather "the naked Other," One whom we yearn for but cannot fully imagine, except as in a glass darkly. Having baptized his imagination with Christian myth years earlier and then having satisfied his intellect, it only remained for Lewis to surrender his will. This was no small task, since he now felt he was not simply accepting a body of doctrines but submitting to a living Person. Christianity is, after all, not simply a philosophy, but a Way.

Jack explained the actual moment of conversion to Christianity in somewhat cryptic terms: "I know very well when, but hardly how, the final step was taken. I was driven to Whipsnade one sunny morning. When we set out I did not believe that Jesus Christ is the Son of God, and when we reached the zoo I did." In the same passage he adds that this was not a particularly emotional moment, nor had he spent the trip in deep contemplation. Rather, he felt like he had awakened from a long sleep and now realized that he was indeed awake.

We know from Warren's diary that this trip took place on September 28, 1931, when Jack was riding in the sidecar of his brother's motorcycle, nine days after his late-night talk with Tolkien and Dyson. Warren wrote in some detail about the outing from the Kilns, their home outside Oxford, to Whipsnade, though he did not know at the time the momentous event that was taking place inside the heart and mind of his brother Jack.

One can't help but wonder, why that particular day? Both Lewis brothers enjoyed visiting the Whipsnade Zoo outside Oxford. It was as much a park as a zoo, with wide, sloping lawns and a magnificent fir wood. The highlight for the two brothers was the bear enclosure and in particular a large, lazy brown bear Jack had dubbed "Mr. Bultitude," after the comical, pompous fellow in F. Anstey's fantasy *Vice Versa* (1882). Jack said that Mr. Bultitude reminded him of "Eden before the Fall," and joked about purchasing the animal as a family pet. No such project was ever pursued in real life, but it was in imagination: in *That Hideous Strength* Mr. Bultitude shows up as a member of Ransom's household at St. Anne's.

The Moores and the Lewis brothers had been planning for some time to drive to the zoo, and this was the appointed day. But the morning had been blanketed in fog, and Maureen argued with her mother at breakfast about whether or not they should cancel the trip. Then there was further discussion and delay about getting the car ready and getting it packed. Warren, unaccustomed to all the fuss and bluster of family life with Minto and Maureen, had gotten increasingly restless and convinced himself that there wasn't going to be time to make the trip. He left the others to their debate and found a quiet place, partly to read a book and partly perhaps to sulk. Then Jack struck a compromise: it was decided that he and Warren should set out for Whipsnade in the motorcycle, Jack in the sidecar, and the others could follow by automobile.

This may not have been an easy decision for Jack. He had mixed feelings about riding in the sidecar of Warren's Daudel. Traveling in any motor vehicle always made him feel he was "annihilating space," and he felt particularly that he had to brace his nerves for a ride on his brother's motorcycle. Here was physical danger, uncertainty, the relinquishing of control—rather too much like diving. Yet there must have been a certain undeniable elation as well. In Lewis's stories, his characters are often forced to accept rides—on sorns, dolphins, owls, galloping steeds, flying horses, even an occasional lion. These daring jaunts are more often than not described in terms suggesting both trepidation and exhilaration.

Whatever his feelings that day, Jack set out with Warren, and the others soon followed. The fog lifted when the two brothers were en route and the sun shone down on the homely cottages and lush fields along the road. In his diary Warren pronounced the outing a success, even though there really hadn't been all that much time to see the zoo. Only long afterward did Warren learn that this was "the most important day in Jack's life," because "it was during that trip that he made a decision to rejoin the Church."

But the question remains, why that particular day? Warren's diary contains not the least hint of anything unusual in his brother's conversation or behavior. Clearly, the road to Whipsnade was not like the one to Damascus. What was happening that day in Jack's mind and heart? Truly, God only knows.

But perhaps one might be permitted to speculate, to enter imaginatively into the moment: They are on the road, finally—Warren on his motorcycle and Jack next to him in the sidecar. The trees and stone walls are whizzing by on either side, but a gray mist veils the horizon and the way ahead. A cool wind is blowing past Jack's face, making his coat flap against his side. Here again is that peculiar thrill of riding, a lightness in the head, a tingle in the stomach—trusting his safety to another.

There is Warnie, old Badger, peering straight ahead, his rounded shoulders hunched forward as he grips the handlebars. Attending church again, after a lapse of many years. Finding truth in the old beliefs. Faith of our fathers. And mothers.

"We few," their band of brothers, all seemed to see it too—Tolkien and Dyson, Coghill, all just like Greeves. Addison's Walk at midnight. Then one. Then two. Talking into the silent, dewy, cobwebby hours of the morning. The Dying God myths, Osiris, Balder—all portraits of Christ. True myth, myth breaking into history. Even Weldon wouldn't deny it. Rum thing. No wish fulfillment there.

The fog is lifting with surprising suddenness, like a door swinging open. There is blue sky overhead. Jack can see down the road now, all the way to the ridge where it curves over the horizon. The sun is shining, like morning, like the first morning of the world. A perfect day for Whipsnade, that little patch of Eden.

Not paradise, of course, only a picture. Like pictures of Joy. This and yet not this. Not a garden isle, not a northern vastness. A face. The face above all worlds. Someone to know and be known by.

But what of freedom? Being "master of my fate, captain of my soul." Nonsense. Poetry for boys. We are not free, not in that sense. Minto, Maureen, Warren. All have much to give, expect much. No more little end room. No sovereignty of solitude.

Lay it down. It's not even yours. It never was. Lay it down as he did. "Except a corn of wheat fall into the ground . . ." Descend and reascend. Like death. Good death. An Anodos who finds his way.

Very well, then, I will ride. Trust my safety to another.

Galilean, God come down from heaven, I believe.

I believe in you.

Teach me to obey.

In Your will is my peace.

EPILOGUE

Lewis's change of heart on the road to Whipsnade took place on September 28, 1931, a month before he turned thirty-three years old. This was just past the midpoint of his life, as he would die November 22, 1963, a week before his sixty-fifth birthday. Yet if it took him longer than most people to hammer out his world-view, the one he forged was one of matchless intellectual vitality and imaginative beauty.

During his teens, Jack had warned Arthur Greeves about the danger of "intellectual stagnation" for those who embraced traditional religious beliefs. But this would not prove to be a problem for Lewis himself. In the first half of his life, his reputation as a writer rested on two slim volumes of poetry, both of which went out of print nearly as soon as they were issued. But the second half of his life brought forth one of the most remarkable writing careers of the twentieth century, a period in which he wrote more than forty books, including acknowledged classics in the fields of Christian apologetics and meditation, science fiction, children's literature and literary scholarship. Lewis's conversion was a watershed event not only because it brought him definitively into the community of faith but also because it resolved a number of other issues he had been grappling with for decades: intellect versus imagination; progress versus regress; spirit versus nature; and self-examination versus self-forgetfulness.

Tolkien and Dyson's paradigm of the incarnation as "True Myth" was indeed good news for Lewis, providing him with the grand synthesis he had been seeking since his Great Bookham days. He had been trapped between an imagination that gloried in nature, myth and romance and an intellect that dismissed it all as a tale told by an idiot, signifying nothing. Besides giving weight and value to myth, this view affirmed the functions of imagination and the intellect to be complementary, not competitive. Lewis would later call imagination "the organ of meaning" and intellect "the organ of truth." The first generates pictures, metaphors and myths by which we understand the world. The second weighs, sifts and analyzes, discerning which products of the imagination correspond most closely with reality.

This view afforded Lewis a tremendous sense of recovery, a method for reembracing what seemed to him his core identity since childhood—wonder, imagination, mythology, faith. With evolutionism such a dominant paradigm in the modern era, it is commonly assumed that change represents progress, that if something is new it must be better. Lewis noted that what past generations would have called permanence, or stability, contemporary thinkers tend to characterize as stagnation. But he also observed that change itself is not growth: "Growth is the synthesis of change and continuity, and where there is no continuity there is no growth." In order to restore continuity, it is sometimes necessary to go back in order to move forward.

In his own life this process began about the time he reached

Oxford, when his interest in materialism and spiritualism began to recede and he began to explore genuinely metaphysical world-views. Lewis's first experience in the renowned university town was a comical one but also, he felt, a deeply significant one. He reports that he came out of the railway station loaded down with luggage and headed down the street in the wrong direction, away from the colleges. He kept walking, increasingly disappointed by the frowzy houses and shops he saw, until he came near to the edge of the city. Only when he saw that he was on the outskirts of town and entering the countryside did he turn around. There spread before him, "never more beautiful since, was the fabled cluster of spires and towers." At that point he realized he had gone the wrong way, turning his back on his true destination. In recounting this episode Lewis concludes that "this little adventure was an allegory of my whole life."

Lewis read this incident as an allegory of his life because it showed that for too long he had been walking in the wrong direction. For him boyhood had been a kind of "fall" from childhood. For him becoming a "grown-up" would be a further step in the wrong direction. Throughout his autobiography, as well as in Lewis's fiction, *grown-up* usually connotes a state of dreary practicality, in which utility and "getting ahead" predominate, or where the sneerings and snobberies of boyhood take on even more sinister manifestations. For him, the path less taken involved a return to a childhood sense of wonder and glory instead of submitting to the mundanities and inanities he found all too prevalent in modern life.

The idea of return meant more to Lewis than just a recovery of childhood. For him the need to look back, or to go back, took many forms: a return to the classics and to neglected authors, to objective moral values, to a traditional Christian understanding of the universe and our place in it. Not surprisingly, Lewis's books abound in metaphors of return, of looking back or going back. As its title suggests, *The Pilgrim's Regress* tells the story of a seeker who finds himself by retracing his steps and discovering the true meaning of his starting point as a child. In *The Great Divorce* Lewis answers Blake's "Marriage of Heaven and Hell" by saying that good comes only by undoing evil, not by trying to wed the two: "I do not think that all who choose wrong roads perish; but their rescue consists in being put back on the right road. A wrong sum can be put right: but only by going back till you find the error and working it afresh from that point, never by simply *going on.* Evil can be undone, but it cannot 'develop' into good. Time does not heal it."

One of the more homespun illustrations of Lewis's principle of moving forward by going back comes in a letter he wrote to Arthur Greeves about humans' view of God's will versus God's view of their will. He asks Arthur to imagine walking his dog on a leash when the dog tries to go around the wrong side of a post and gets his leash caught in a loop. The owner sees that the dog is stuck and tries to pull him back so that he can continue to walk forward. The dog thinks the only way to go forward is to keep pulling his leash straight ahead. If he is an obedient dog, he may reluctantly give in, not realizing that he and his owner both want the same thing. Lewis goes on to say that if the dog were a theologian, he would label his attempts to go forward as a temptation to sin and would have to learn to surrender his will. The only way he could truly understand would be if the owner could address the animal, "My dear dog," and explain that his own will must be denied so that he may resume his true progress forward.

As opposed to the ethic of evolutionism, where life is always pressing forward and where cultural progress is inevitable, Lewis argues that sometimes one must simply turn and go back—to recover what has been lost, to reclaim "the truth in old books," sometimes even to repent. He felt much the same way about metaphysics, as he explains in *Miracles:*

> Only Supernaturalists really see Nature. You must go a little away from her, and then turn round, and look back. Then at last the true landscape will become visible. You must have tasted, however briefly, the pure water from beyond the world before you can be distinctly conscious of the hot, salty tang of Nature's current. To treat her as God, or as Everything, is to lose the whole pith and pleasure of her. Come out, look back, and then you will see.

Besides illustrating his doctrine of moving forward by going back, this passage also shows how Lewis eventually resolved his prolonged inquiry into the relations of spirit and nature. As a materialist he had tried to deny the reality of an immaterial realm altogether. As a dualist he had viewed the human spirit at war with the material world. As an Idealist he had pondered a Universal Spirit immanent in nature. Finally, as a Christian he would view God as Spirit—the supreme Spirit—not in nature or against it, but above it—its Creator. In this view humans need not spurn nature as evil or worship it as divine, but rather to value nature as a part of creation as we ourselves are. As Lewis explained the Christian view succinctly, "God never meant man to be a purely spiritual creature. That is why He uses material things like bread and wine to put the new life into us. We may think this rather crude and unspiritual. God does not: he invented eating. He likes matter. He invented it."

For Lewis, his newfound Christian faith enabled him to be in right relation with God, with nature, with others and with himself. As discussed in previous chapters, he grew up with a habit of intense self-scrutiny, a tendency to watch his own mind at work. In

his youth, when psychoanalysis was in its heyday, frequent introspection was considered healthy and necessary to sort out re-
pressed conflicts or unconscious desires. But after the collapse and
death of his friend Doc Askins, Lewis came more and more to associate introspection and self-analysis with narcissism and neurosis.

In *Surprised by Joy* Lewis reports that after his theistic conversion in 1929, he experienced a noticeable decrease "in the fussy
attentiveness which I had so long paid to the progress of my own
opinions and the states of my own mind." He adds that while for
many becoming converted might lead to greater self-examination, the opposite was true for him. His ideal became self-forgetfulness, so that introspection was to be used for practical
purposes at specified times, "a duty, a discipline, an uncomfortable thing, no longer a hobby or a habit." For Lewis this was a
definite turn toward greater emotional health: "To believe and to
pray were the beginning of extroversion. I had been, as they say,
'taken out of my self.' "

This change from self-scrutiny to self-forgetfulness in Lewis was
apparent even to his friends. His friend Owen Barfield reports that
"at a certain stage in his life [Jack] deliberately ceased to take any
interest in himself except as a kind of spiritual alumnus taking his
moral finals." Barfield felt that this began as a deliberate choice
and developed into an ingrained habit of mind, a sense that, to
avoid "spiritual megalomania," self-scrutiny should limit itself
mainly to recognizing one's own weaknesses and shortcomings.
This sounds a bit condescending on Barfield's part, but Lewis
would probably have agreed. After all, he is the one who wrote in
The Screwtape Letters that the very mark of hell is a "ruthless,
sleepless, unsmiling concentration on the self."

Ironically, the only way to produce a thought-provoking book such as *The Screwtape Letters,* the work which first brought Lewis international acclaim, was to engage in that very kind of ruthless self-examination. As he explained in the 1961 preface to the book:

> Some have paid me an undeserved compliment by supposing that my *Letters* were the ripe fruit of many years' study in moral and ascetic theology. They forgot that there is an equally reliable, though less creditable, way of learning how temptation works. "My heart"— I need no other's—"sheweth me the wickedness of the ungodly."

When he became a Christian, Lewis set aside introspection as self-therapy, but he took it up as philosophy. One of those "practical purposes" he spoke of for self-examination was to study how the workings of his own mind shed light on the nature of reality. Especially since the time of John Locke in the seventeenth century, Western philosophers have increasingly devoted themselves to examining the contents of human consciousness. Bishop Berkeley, for example, stated explicitly that he intended to critique empiricism by "looking a little into one's own thoughts, and by examining the ideas or images found there."

Lewis was well trained in philosophy, and he adapted this method effectively in his works of Christian apologetics and meditation. While other defenders of Christian faith have stressed the intelligent design of the cosmos, the historicity of Gospel records, the fulfillment of Bible prophecies or the transformation of individual lives, Lewis focuses instead on the workings of human minds and human cultures. His most oft-repeated arguments for Christianity—universal moral values, an equally universal sense of not living up to those values, the experience of Joy, the prevalence of Dying God myths—all of these hark back to human consciousness for a clearer understanding of fundamental realities.

The issue of self-examination versus self-forgetfulness in Lewis's life is filled with paradoxes. For one thing, he felt that in becoming a Christian he was able to move away from his habit of ceaseless introspection. Yet his ability to attend so carefully to his own inner world is what makes him such a perceptive commentator on his readers' foibles and failures, and also on their sources of awe, hope and faith.

In another paradox the young Lewis was fascinated in his teens by the topic of paranormal experiences, by accounts of those whose visions, premonitions or clairvoyant episodes had allegedly carried their consciousness beyond the frontiers of space and time. Then in the last year of his life, when he had put away boyish things and showed little interest in the paranormal, he seems to have had the kind of experience that he was so hungry to know about a half century earlier.

Walter Hooper reports that in the last months of Lewis's life, after he had already suffered from a heart attack and coma in July 1963, his health continued to be delicate, with episodes of mental disorientation. One afternoon when he was still convalescing in a local nursing home in Oxford, Lewis woke up from a nap and asked Hooper for a glass of water. As Hooper went to a basin at the side of the bed, Lewis suddenly pulled himself up and stared intently across the room. Hooper saw nothing but felt that Jack must have seen something or someone "very great and beautiful" near at hand, for there was a rapturous expression on his face unlike anything Hooper had seen before. Jack kept on looking, and repeated to himself several times, "Oh, I never imagined, I never imagined." The joyous expression remained on his features as he fell back onto his pillows and went to sleep. Later on he remembered nothing of this episode, but he said that even speculating about it with Hooper gave him a "refreshment of the spirit." Whatever the meaning of such an incident, it seems highly appropriate that this experience, like Joy itself, should visit Lewis when he least sought it.

A final paradox lies in Lewis's probing self-examination of his own motives for writing. Back in 1930, during his spiritual apprenticeship when he considered himself a theist but not yet a Christian, Jack wrote a candid letter to Arthur Greeves, who harbored literary ambitions of his own. In one of those self-directed sermons which he sometimes wrote to Arthur, Lewis argues at length that the desire to achieve greatness as a writer was an idol that needed to be given up, a sacrifice which, if accepted as death, could become the beginning of new life. In the same letter he declares that literary ambition was a kind of disease from which they both should seek deliverance. He says that one cannot help longing to write, to get one's thoughts and feelings down on paper, but that writing to seek acclaim was an unworthy motive that must be overcome. He thinks it would be better for both of them if they learned this early on, that if God did not cauterize this infection at that time, they would have to face a more severe treatment later on. He concludes that there can be a positive pleasure in setting aside one's prideful dreams:

> And, honestly, the being cured, with all the pain, has pleasure too: one creeps home, tired and bruised, into a state of mind that is really restful, when all one's ambitions have been given up. Then one can really for the first time say "Thy Kingdom come": for in that Kingdom there will be no pre-eminences and a man must have reached a stage of not caring two straws about his own status before he can enter it.

The following year, by his own account, Lewis entered into that kingdom, declaring that Jesus Christ is God. By the end of his life he had published forty books, and another twenty books of his writings have been published posthumously. In the last decade his books have been selling at a rate of several million copies a year, and just about every scrap of paper on which he scribbled a few lines has become a serious candidate for publication—including private letters in which he earnestly declared his desire to be delivered from the yearning for eminence.

From Lewis's own writings we can see that he eventually came to regard literary success a secondary matter. The real story of Lewis's conversion, then, is not about dramatic changes in a man's career, but about dramatic changes in the man. Many writers are able to create winsome personas in their books, even when their personal lives reflect little of the wisdom, serenity or healthy-mindedness found in their works. But most who knew Lewis in his later years agree that the person they met face to face was very similar to the one they encountered in the pages of his books.

Walter Hooper speaks for many when he observes of Jack that "he was the most thoroughly converted man I ever met." After a long journey of many years, the pilgrim learned how to blend incisiveness of mind with singleness of heart. As many who knew him have attested, Lewis in the second half of his life seems to have been one of those rare souls who could combine goodness and greatness.

Lewis wrote a treatise defending miracles, but perhaps his own life makes the point more eloquently than his book. For it was the brilliant young atheist, a "most reluctant convert" halfway through his life, who was destined to become the most highly regarded Christian writer of his generation. Surely, he never imagined, he never imagined.

Abbreviations of Lewis's Works

AF	Autobiographical fragment (58 pages) composed about 1930. Unpublished manuscript available at the Marion E. Wade Center, Wheaton College, Wheaton, Illinois.
AL	*The Allegory of Love*. 1936. Reprint, London: Oxford University Press, 1973.
AM	*The Abolition of Man*. 1943. Reprint, New York: Macmillan, 1973.
AMR	*All My Road Before Me: The Diary of C. S. Lewis, 1922-1927*. Edited by Walter Hooper. San Diego: Harcourt Brace Jovanovich, 1991.
CR	*Christian Reflections*. Edited by Walter Hooper. Grand Rapids, Mich.: Eerdmans, 1973.
DI	*The Discarded Image*. 1964. Reprint, Cambridge: Cambridge University Press, 1971.
Dy	*Dymer*. 1926. Reprint, New York: Macmillan, 1950.
EC	*An Experiment in Criticism*. Cambridge: Cambridge University Press, 1961.
EL	*English Literature in the Sixteenth Century, Excluding Drama*. Oxford: Clarendon, 1954.
FE	*Fern-Seed and Elephants and Other Essays on Christianity*. Edited by Walter Hooper. New York: Collins/Fountain, 1977.
FL	*The Four Loves*. New York: Harcourt Brace Jovanovich, 1960.
GD	*The Great Divorce*. 1946. Reprint, New York: Fontana, 1972.
GITD	*God in the Dock: Essays on Theology and Ethics*. Edited by Walter Hooper. Grand Rapids, Mich.: Eerdmans, 1970.
GM	*George Macdonald: An Anthology*. Edited by C. S. Lewis. Garden City, N.Y.: Doubleday, 1962.
GO	*A Grief Observed*. London: Faber & Faber, 1961.

HHB   *The Horse and His Boy.* 1954. Reprint, New York: Collier/Macmillan, 1970.

LAL   *Letters to an American Lady.* Edited by Clyde S. Kilby. Grand Rapids, Mich.: Eerdmans, 1967.

LB   *The Last Battle.* 1956. Reprint, New York: Collier/Macmillan, 1970.

LCSL   *Letters of C. S. Lewis.* Edited, with a memoir, by W. H. Lewis. New York: Harcourt Brace Jovanovich, 1966.

LDGC   *Letters: C. S. Lewis/Don Giovanni Calabria.* Translated and edited by Martin Moynihan. Ann Arbor, Mich.: Servant, 1989.

LM   *Letters to Malcolm: Chiefly on Prayer.* New York: Harcourt Brace Jovanovich, 1964.

LP   Lewis, Warren H., ed. "The Lewis Papers: The Memoirs of the Lewis Family, 1850-1930." Oxford: Leeborough Press, 1933. 11 vols. Unpublished bound papers, Marion E. Wade Center, Wheaton College, Wheaton, Illinois.

LRev   *Letters of C. S. Lewis.* Edited, with a memoir, by W. H. Lewis. Revised and enlarged by Walter Hooper. London: Harper Collins, 1988.

LTC   *Letters to Children.* Edited by Lyle W. Dorsett and Marjorie Lamp Mead. New York: Macmillan, 1985.

LWW   *The Lion, the Witch, and the Wardrobe.* 1950. Reprint, New York: Collier/Macmillan, 1970.

MC   *Mere Christianity.* 1952. Reprint, New York: Macmillan, 1969.

MN   *The Magician's Nephew.* 1955. Reprint, New York: Collier/Macmillan, 1970.

Mir   *Miracles: A Preliminary Study.* 1947. Reprint, New York: Macmillan, 1968.

NP   *Narrative Poems.* Edited by Walter Hooper. London: Geoffrey Bles, 1969.

OOW   *Of Other Worlds: Essays and Stories.* Edited by Walter Hooper. New York: Harcourt Brace Jovanovich, 1975.

OS   *On Stories and Other Essays on Literature.* New York: Harcourt Brace Jovanovich, 1982.

OSP   *Out of the Silent Planet.* 1938. Reprint, New York: Macmillan, 1968.

P   *Poems.* Edited by Walter Hooper. New York: Harcourt Brace Jovanovich, 1964.

PCa   *Prince Caspian.* 1951. Reprint, New York: Collier/Macmillan, 1970.

PCo   *Present Concerns.* Edited by Walter Hooper. San Diego: Harcourt Brace Jovanovich, 1987.

Per   *Perelandra.* 1943. Reprint, New York: Macmillan, 1968.

PH   *The Personal Heresy: A Controversy.* 1939. Reprint, London: Oxford University Press, 1965.

PP   *The Problem of Pain.* 1940. Reprint, London: Collins, 1972.

PPL   *A Preface to Paradise Lost.* 1942. Reprint, London: Oxford University Press, 1970.

PR   *The Pilgrim's Regress.* 1933. Reprint, New York: Harcourt Brace Jovanovich, 1960.

ROE   *Rehabilitations and Other Essays.* London: Oxford University Press, 1939.

RP   *Reflections on the Psalms.* 1958. Reprint, New York: Harcourt Brace Jovanovich, 1982.

SB   *Spirits in Bondage: A Cycle of Lyrics.* 1919. Reprint, New York: Harcourt Brace Jovanovich, 1984.

SBJ   *Surprised by Joy: The Shape of My Early Life.* New York: Harcourt Brace Jovanovich, 1955.

SC   *The Silver Chair.* 1953. Reprint, New York: Collier/Macmillan, 1970.

SIL   *Spenser's Images of Life.* Edited by Alistair Fowler. Cambridge: Cambridge University Press, 1967.

SL   *The Screwtape Letters.* 1942. Reprint, New York: Macmillan, 1960.

SLE   *Selected Literary Essays.* Edited by Walter Hooper. Cambridge: Cambridge University Press, 1966.

SMRL   *Studies in Medieval and Renaissance Literature.* Edited by Walter Hooper. Cambridge: Cambridge University Press, 1969.

SPT   *Screwtape Proposes a Toast and Other Pieces.* London: Collins, 1970.

SW   *Studies in Words.* Cambridge: Cambridge University Press, 1960.

THS   *That Hideous Strength: A Modern Fairy-Tale for Grown-Ups.*

	1945. Reprint, New York: Macmillan, 1968.
TST	*They Stand Together: The Letters of C. S. Lewis to Arthur Greeves (1914-1963)*. Edited by Walter Hooper. New York: Macmillan, 1979.
TWHF	*Till We Have Faces*. 1956. Reprint, Grand Rapids, Mich.: Eerdmans, 1966.
VDT	*The Voyage of the "Dawn Treader."* New York: Collier/Macmillan, 1970.
WG	*The Weight of Glory and Other Addresses*. 1949. Reprint, Grand Rapids, Mich.: Eerdmans, 1965.
WLN	*The World's Last Night and Other Essays*. New York: Harcourt Brace Jovanovich, 1960.

Notes

Introduction

Page 11: "I believe in no religion": *TST* 135.

Page 11: "Christianity is God expressing himself": *TST* 427-28.

Page 11: "Never sank so low as to pray": Baker, p. 6.

Page 11: "You take too many things for granted": Baker, p. 4.

Page 12: "The most dejected and reluctant convert": *SBJ* 228-29.

Page 12: Most widely recognized after Churchill: Como, p. xxi.

Page 12: Sales of six million copies a year: Graham A. Cole, "C. S. Lewis: An Evangelical Appreciation," *The Reformed Theological Review* 53, no. 3 (1994): 102.

Page 13: "Passed from Atheism to Christianity": *SBJ* vii.

Chapter 1: The Ill-Secured Happiness of Childhood

Page 19: "He is Jacksie": *LCSL* 2.

Page 20: Jack's first view of the sea: Warren Lewis, *Biography*, p. 4.

Page 20: "You cannot see things": *OSP* 42.

Page 20: Civilization had not died or slumbered: *EL* 20.

Page 20: Looking up at the Heavens: *DI* 33, 111.

Page 20: "For what you see and hear": *MN* 125.

Page 21: Differing views of Thomas and Mary Hamilton: Sayer, p. 5.

Page 22: Albert Lewis's Anti-Home Rule speech: *LP* 4:13-14.

Page 22: Flora Lewis hires Catholic domestic workers: Sayer, p. 10.

Page 22: Flora Lewis comments on Orangemen: *LP* 3:120.

Page 22: "Politics and money": *LCSL* 6.

Page 22: Lewis's disdain for politics: *LCSL* 6.

Page 23: "A deep-seated spiritual illness": *LCSL* 19.

Page 23: "Knew not by what spirit": *LDGC* 83.

Page 23: Lewis stresses Welsh and English origins: *SBJ* 3; Sayer, p. 4.

Page 24: Warren Hamilton Lewis's books are *The Splendid Century: Some Aspects of French Life in the Reign of Louis XIV* (London: Eyre & Spottiswood, 1953); *The Sunset of the Splendid Century: The Life and Times of Louis Auguste de Bour-*

bon, Duc de Maine, 1670-1736 (London: Eyre & Spottiswood, 1955); *Assault on Olympus: The Rise of the House of Gramont Between 1604 and 1678* (London: André Deutsch, 1958); *Louis XIV: An Informal Portrait* (London: André Deutsch, 1959); *The Scandalous Regent: A Life of Phillippe, Duc d'Orleans, 1674-1723, and of His Family* (London: André Deutsch, 1961); *Levantine Adventurer: The Travels and Missions of the Chevalier d'Arvieux, 1653-1697* (London: André Deutsch, 1962); *Memoirs of the Duc de Saint-Simon* (London: B. T. Batsford, 1964).

Page 24:   "True Welshmen" versus "a cooler race": *SBJ* 3.

Page 24:   Sayer demurs from former mentor: Sayer, p. 5.

Page 25:   Flora's letter to Albert Lewis: *LP* 2:300.

Page 25:   Sharp contrast between parents' temperaments: *SBJ* 4.

Page 25:   *Paradise Lost* 4.370.

Page 26:   Recollections of Lizzie Endicott: *SBJ* 5.

Page 26:   "Unless we return": *CR* 81.

Page 26:   Jane Studdock at St. Anne's: *THS* 30.

Page 26:   "I'm not a bucking nurse": *THS* 111.

Page 27:   Jack and Warren's reading and writing: *SBJ* 14-15.

Page 27:   Anxiety about ghosts and insects: *SBJ* 9.

Page 27:   Tiger or a ghost in the next room: *PP* 5.

Page 27:   "Say a child's prayer": *Per* 171.

Page 28:   "Nearer by twenty centuries": *EL* 26-27.

Page 28:   "Pure and momentous spiritual experiences": *PP* 67.

Page 28:   "Something cool, fresh, dewy, exuberant": *SBJ* 7.

Page 28:   "Unsatisfied desire": *SBJ* 17-18.

Page 28:   Joy as always "over there": *AF* 5.

Page 29:   Lines from Longfellow: *SBJ* 17.

Page 29:   "Northernness": *SBJ* 17.

Page 29:   "A votary of the Blue Flower": *SBJ* 7.

Page 30:   Bereavement began before Flora Lewis's death: *SBJ* 18-19.

Page 30:   "Bad temper": *LP* 3:89.

Page 31:   "Christianity is not a patent medicine": *GITD* 108-9.

Page 31:   "Distortions in character": *GM* 13.

Page 31:   "Anti-Freudian predicament": *GM* 14.

Page 32:   Freud's theories have been widely questioned: See Malcolm Macmillan, *Freud Evaluated: The Completed Arc* (New York: North-Holland, 1991); Allen Esterson, *The Seductive Mirage: An Exploration of the Work of Sigmund Freud* (New York: Open Court, 1993); John Kerr, *A Most Dangerous Method: The Story of Jung, Freud, and Sabina Speilrein* (New York: Alfred Knopf, 1993); Adolf Grunbaum, *Validation in the Clinical Theory of Psychoanalysis* (Madison, Conn: International Universities Press, 1992); Frederick Crews, "The Unknown Freud," *New York Times*

Review of Books, November 18, 1993, pp. 55-66.

Page 32:   "A double-edged sword": Paul Vitz, *Faith of the Fatherless: The Psychology of Atheism* (Dallas: Thomas Spence, 1999), p. 4.

Page 32:   "Atheism of the strong type": Vitz 3.

Page 33:   "With my mother's death": *SBJ* 21.9.

Chapter 2: The Alien Territory of Boyhood

Page 35:   Misery of school clothes: *SBJ* 22.

Page 36:   English accents: *SBJ* 24.

Page 36:   "Even in 1905": *LP* 3:33-35.

Page 36:   Working the same four sums: Sayer, p. 26.

Page 36:   Court action against Capron: Green & Hooper, p. 26.

Page 37:   Memories confirmed by others: Kilby & Mead, p. 247.

Page 37:   Oldie later certified as insane: Green & Hooper, p. 28.

Page 37:   Lewis finally forgave the man: *LAL* 117.

Page 37:   "Is always too hard": *SBJ* 30.

Page 37:   Flora saw Wynyard firsthand: *LP* 3:32, 35.

Page 37:   "Friction between a master and his pupils": *LP* 3:109.

Page 38:   Flora never thought such a thing: *LP* 3:95.

Page 38:   "An infernal hog": *LP* 3:147.

Page 38:   Jack's pleas to leave Wynyard: *LP* 3:147.

Page 38:   "A coward and a crybaby": *SBJ* 31.

Page 38:   "He would rather represent his master": *SBJ* 31.

Page 39:   Description of Uncle Andrew: *MN* 4:11.

Page 39:   Andrew has turned sixty: *MN* 112.

Page 39:   Similar smiles: *LP* 3:41; *MN* 12, 23, 24.

Page 39:   Forgotten quest for Joy: *SBJ* 34.

Page 39:   Children's stories versus school stories: *SBJ* 35.

Page 40:   Curiosity of children versus interests of schoolboys: *SBJ* 35.

Page 40:   "Alien territory": *SBJ* 71-72.

Page 40:   "We are obliged to go": Warren Lewis, *Biography,* p. 21.

Page 41:   "Was I not an Ulster Protestant": *SBJ* 33.

Page 41:   "Bishops not beer": *SLE* 122.

Page 41:   "Moral severity": *EL* 42-44.

Page 41:   "The life of 'religion' ": *EL* 42.

Page 41:   "Apostate Puritans": *SBJ* 69.

Page 41:   "*Memory* of Christianity": *TST* 433.

Page 42:   "I dreamed of a boy": *PR* 20.

Chapter 3: Mere Atheism in Early Adolescence

Page 55:   Millions of miles cannot be imagined: *DI* 98.

Page 55:   Physical size no measure of spiritual value: *GITD* 41.

Page 56:   "The size and emptiness of the universe": *PP* 141-42.

Page 56:   Kirkpatrick's letter to Albert Lewis: *LP* 3:119.

Page 57:   "You ask me my religious views": *TST* 135.

Page 58:   "I am quite content": *TST* 137-38.

Page 58:   "Exulted with youthful pride": *SBJ* 173.

Page 59:   "Our future home down below": *TST* 73.

Page 59:   Elders bowing on a sea of glass: *TST* 72.

Page 59:   "The luminous ignorance of youth": *TST* 107.

Page 59:   "With the confidence of a boy": *SBJ* 204.

Page 60:   Weston and Devine before an eldil: *OSP* 126.

Page 60:   Dwarves who can't see the New Narnia: *LB* 147.

Page 60:   "Looking along the beam": *GITD* 212.

Page 61:   "In other words, you can stand outside": *GITD* 215.

Page 61:   "Bundles of complexes": *GITD* 271-72.

Page 62:   "But you cannot go on 'explaining away' for ever": *AM* 91.

Chapter 4: The Dungeon of a Divided Soul

Page 63:   Poetry and myth versus rationalism: *SBJ* 170.

Page 64:   "Great literary experience": *TST* 92.

Page 64:   "Spiritual healing, of being washed": *TST* 389.

Page 64:   "Cool faithfulness": George MacDonald, *Phantastes and Lilith* (Grand Rapids, Mich.: Eerdmans, 1964), p. 39.

Page 64:   "Capacity for simple happiness": MacDonald, p. 43.

Page 65:   "A blessing, like the kiss of a mother": MacDonald, p. 128.

Page 65:   "Dreams of unspeakable joy": MacDonald, p. 129.

Page 65:   "I was dead, and right content": MacDonald, pp. 177-78.

Page 65:   "A power of calm endurance": MacDonald, p. 180.

Page 65:   "Yet I know that good is coming": MacDonald, p. 182.

Page 66:   "Crossed a great frontier": *GM* 25.

Page 66:   "A sort of cool, morning innocence": *GM* 26.

Page 66:   "Did nothing to my intellect": *GM* 26.

Page 66:   "The quality which had enchanted me": *GM* 26-27.

Page 67:   All summary and quotations from C. S. Lewis's "The Quest of Bleheris" are taken from an unpublished manuscript in the Bodleian Library, Oxford (MS. Eng. lett. c. 220/5 fols. 5-43). Copies are available at the Marion E. Wade Center, Wheaton College. The manuscript is not consistently paginated, so page numbers are not cited. Minor errors of spelling and punctuation have been corrected.

Page 69:   Effect of Aslan's name: *LWW* 64.

Page 70:   Not making fun of Christianity: *TST* 124.

Page 70:   "Mad Parson" Straik: *THS* 78-80.

Page 72:   Hyperites as a Christ figure: Sayer, p. 60.

Page 72:   Greek meaning of Hyperites: Henry Liddell and George Scott, *A Greek-English Lexicon* (Oxford: Clarendon, 1919), p. 1609.

Page 73:   "I may fall, but while I live": *OSP* 137.

Page 73:   J. B. S. Haldane, "Auld Hornie, F. R. S.," *Modern Quarterly* 1 (Autumn 1946): 32-40. Reprinted in *Shadows of Imagination: The Fantasies of C. S. Lewis, J. R. R. Tolkien, and Charles Williams,* ed. Mark R. Hillegas (Carbondale, Ill.: Southern Illinois University Press, 1969).

Page 74:   Lewis on why he never became a leftist: *SBJ* 173.

Page 75:   Idea of autumn as catalyst for Joy: *SBJ* 16.

Page 76:   "There are only two kinds of people in the end": *GD* 72.

Page 78:   "Most obviously a quest for the deity": Sayer, p. 60.

Page 78:   All human loves are mere copies: *PR* 67-68.

Page 78:   "Spilt religion": *PR* 11.

Page 78:   "I think Bleheris has killed my muse": *TST* 107.

Page 79:   "As to Bleheris, he is dead": *TST* 136.

Chapter 5: Dualism During the War Years

Page 81:   "Youth and age touch only the surface": *THS* 21.

Page 82:   Jack was Kirkpatrick's most accomplished student: *SB* xxii.

Page 83:   "Still moving like half-crushed beetles": *SBJ* 196.

Page 84:   "I know that you will come and see me": *LP* 5:330-31.

Page 84:   Jack's letter about Mrs. Moore: *LP* 5:330-31.

Page 85:   "Jack has been so good to me": *LP* 4:44-45.

Page 85:   "It is four months now": *LP* 6:17-18.

Page 86:   Letter suggesting they poison "old Stokes": *TST* 97.

Page 86:   Warren on their father's interference: *LCSL* 7.

Page 86:   Jack introducing Mrs. Moore as his mother: *LCSL* 12.

Page 86:   "He had lost his mother": Ann Bonsor, " 'One Huge and Complex Episode': The Diary of C. S. Lewis," *The Contemporary Review,* March 1992, p. 145.

Page 87:   "Lovers": Wilson, p. 58.

Page 87:   "Friend and companion": Hooper, *Guide,* p. 712; *AMR* 9.

Page 87:   Chances of a sexual element: Sayer, p. 89.

Page 87:   Readers prefer gossip: *PH* 28.

Page 87:   "French Nocturne": *SB* 47.

Page 88:   War experiences cut off from the rest of his life: *SBJ* 196.

Page 88:   "Satan Speaks": *SB* 3.

Page 89:   Fenris Ulf: This character's name in British editions, and in the new Harper Collins editions of the Narnia Chronicles (1994), is given as Maugrim.

Page 89:   "De Profundis": *SB* 20-21.

Page 89:   "Ode for a New Year's Day": *SB* 14-15.

Page 90:   "No useful purpose is served": *SB* xxxvii.

Page 90:   "[Jack] is young and will learn in time" *SB* xxxviii.

Page 90:   Albert doesn't want the book left out in plain sight: Baker, p. 5.

Page 90:   Jack says he's not denouncing the Christian God: Sayer, p. 85.

Page 91:   "Spirit continually dodging matter": *TST* 214.

Page 91:   "Puritan practice": *TST* 221.

Page 91:   The beauty in a tree: *TST* 217.

Page 91:   "Matter's great enemy": *TST* 217.

Page 92:   "Talk was saturated": *TST* 234.

Page 92:   "Nature is wholly diabolical & malevolent": *TST* 230.

Page 93:   Jack was not temperamentally gloomy: Warren Lewis, *Biography, p. 270.*

Page 93:   "The snares that lurk about the word *Nothing*": *SBJ* 198.

Page 93:   Schopenhauer's "haunting idea": *SBJ* 204.

Page 94:   Critique of Schopenhauer: Henri Bergson, *Creative Evolution*, trans. Arthur Mitchell (New York: Modern Library, 1944), pp. 305-7.

Page 94:   "The wisest and best of my unofficial teachers": Dedication to *The Allegory of Love* (1936).

Page 94:   "Rock-bottom reality": *SBJ* 208.

Page 94:   "Seeing, listening, smelling, receptive creature": *SBJ* 199.

Page 94:   "Very quiddity of the thing": *SBJ* 199.

Page 95:   *Phantastes* as a devotional book: *AMR* 177.

Page 95:   "Visitation[s] of Joy": *SBJ* 181.

Chapter 6: "Spiritual Lust" & the Lure of the Occult

Page 101:   "A foolish consistency": Ralph Waldo Emerson, "Self-Reliance," paragraph 13.

Page 101:   Lewis's materialistic "faith" began to waver: *SBJ* 174.

Page 102:   Atheism and occultism insulate against Christian faith: *SBJ* 66.

Page 102:   Lewis's "magical excursions": *AF* 39.

Page 102:   "Upon a firm foundation": *CR* 59.

Page 103:   "Floundering in the mazes": *SBJ* 59.

Page 103:   Helena Blavatsky: Richard Ellman, *Yeats: The Man and the Masks* (New York: E. P. Dutton, 1948), p. 57.

Page 104:   "Scarred his mind for life": Patrick Mahony, *Maurice Maeterlinck: Mystic and Dramatist* (Washington D.C.: Institute for the Study of Man, 1984), p. 9.

Page 104:   "The phenomena are certainly extraordinary": *TST* 1894.

Page 105:   Members of the SPR: William F. Barrett, F. R. S. Psychical Research (New York: Henry Holt, 1911), p. 41.

Page 105:   "The obvious fact": Frederick W. H. Myers, *Science and a Future Life* (London: Macmillan, 1893), p. 4.

Page 106:   Spiritual phenomena would become accepted: Myers, pp. 41-42.

Page 106:   "The facts": Oliver J. Lodge, *Raymond, or Life After Death* (New York: George H. Doran, 1916), pp. 84-85.

Page 107:   Skepticism impedes loved ones from making contact: Lodge, p. 87.

Page 108:   "They will reveal": Barrett, p. 10.

Page 108:   Wife's vision of her wounded husband: Barrett, pp. 122-23.

Page 108:   Other cases of remote sensing: Barrett, pp. 126-31.

Page 108:   The C. W. Sanders case: Barrett, pp. 161-65; see also G. W. Mitchell, *X + Y = Z; or The Sleeping Preacher* (New York: W. C. Smith, 1876).

Page 110:   Jane Studdock's unwanted gift of dreaming realities: *THS* 65, 115.

Page 110:   King Tirian's vision: *LB* 42.

Page 110:   Lewis might have ended up a Satanist or a madman: *SBJ* 176.

Page 111:   "Promises to exclude the bogies": *SBJ* 177.

Page 111:   "A wholesome antipathy": *SBJ* 178.

Page 111:   Yeats's dream of becoming a wizard: Ellman, pp. 4, 25-27.

Page 112:   "Come along": *LRev* 122.

Page 112:   Letters about visits with Yeats: *LP* 6:262; *LRev* 123; *TST* 286.

Page 113:   Blake's most famous etching: Robert N. Essick, *William Blake, Printmaker* (Princeton, N.J.: Princeton University Press, 1980), illus. p. 221.

Page 113:   "Wicked"; "diabolical": *LRev* 123; *TST* 286.

Page 114:   MacGregor Matthews: Ellman, pp. 92-93.

Page 114:   "The most eloquent drunk Irishman": *LRev* 125.

Page 114:   "Sham romance": *LP* 6:262.

Page 114:   Reverend F. W. Macran: *AMR* 467.

Page 114:   "An old, dirty, gabbling Irish parson": *SBJ* 201.

Page 115:   "Why people in his position": *AMR* 22.

Page 115:   "I wonder if mastodons": *AMR* 22.

Page 115:   "Mocker"; "atheistical dog": *LRev* 123.

Page 115:   "Not between high and low": *LRev* 327.

Page 116:   "Hold him while he kicked": *SBJ* 203.

Page 116:   "The beaten track": *SBJ* 203.

Page 116:   "Ready-made orthodoxy": *AMR* 41, 48.

Page 116:   "If you stopped to think": *AMR* 135.

Page 116:   "Satanic badness": *AMR* 191-92.

Page 117:   Askins's final breakdown: *AMR* 202-18.

Page 117:   Possession disorder: See Chadwick Hansen, *Witchcraft at Salem* (New York: Braziller, 1985); David C. Downing, "The Mystery of Spirit Possession," *Books and Culture,* January/February 1997, pp. 17-20; T. Craig Isaacs, "The Possession States Disorder," Ph.D. diss, abstract in *Dissertation Abstracts International* 46 (1986): 4403.

Page 117:   "Keep clear of introspection": *TST* 292.

Page 117:   "It would be difficult to exaggerate": *TST* 293n.

Page 118:   "Eden fields long lost to man": *Dy* 7.7.

Page 118:   "Spirits in the dust": *Dy* 7.8.

Page 118:   "Scream alone": *Dy* 7.9.

Page 118:   Jack recommends books on psychic research: *TST* 189.

Page 118:   "Great magician" Cornelius Agrippa: *TST* 191.

Page 118:   Shakespeare's conjurer and skeptic: *King Henry IV, Part I,* 3.1.53-56.

Page 119:   "People shouldn't call for demons": *LB* 82-83.

Page 119:   "I call that force into me": *Per* 96.

Page 119:   "Often its grimaces": *Per* 129.

Page 119:   "A man I had loved dearly": *SBJ* 202.

Page 119:   "Seize a grand role": *Per* 133.

Page 119:   Hideous truths: *Per* 170.

Page 119:   Fascination for spiritualism hastened Doc's collapse: *AMR* 221.

Page 120:   Merlin is a soul in need of saving: *THS* 289.

Page 120:   "Laying his mind open": *THS* 285.

Page 120:   "High and lonely destiny": *MN* 18.

Page 120:   "There is something which unites": *AM* 87-88.

Page 121:   "It is the very mark": *WG* 63.

Page 121:   "Are equally pleased": *SL* 9.

Chapter 7: Idealism & Pantheism in the Twenties

Page 123:   "On the intellectual side": *PR* 5.

Page 125:   "The fuller splendor behind the sensuous curtain": *SBJ* 210.

Page 125:   "To prove the existence of God": *TST* 196.

Page 125:   Berkeley limericks: Bertrand Russell, *History of Western Philosophy* (London: Allen & Unwin, 1967), p. 623.

Page 126:   "Creative Evolution" mentioned in *Perelandra: Per* 121.

Page 126:   "One wants to be careful": *Per* 93.

Page 127:   Green, Bradley, and Bosanquet as "mighty names": *SBJ* 209.

Page 127:   The "dynasty" that most shaped Lewis's Idealism: *PR* 5.

Page 127:   "The vehicle of an eternally complete consciousness": *Prolegomena,* p. 72. Quoted in Frederick Copleston, S.J., *A History of Philosophy: Volume Three, Bentham to Russell* (Westminster, Md.: Newman, 1966), p. 169.

Page 127:   "Vague and woolly speculation": Copleston, p. 171.

Page 128:   Bradley scorned nineteenth-century empiricism: Richard Waldheim, *F. H. Bradley* (Baltimore, Md.: Penguin, 1969), p. 12. See also *The Philosophy of F. H. Bradley,* ed. Anthony Manser and Guy Stock (Oxford: Clarendon, 1984).

Page 128:   Bradley envisioned an all-embracing Absolute: Copleston, p. 209.

Page 128:   "Metaphysics is the finding of bad reasons": Copleston, p. 213.

Page 129:   "Only two serious philosophical options": *CR* 71.

Page 129:   Pantheism is actually an age-old religion: *Mir* 84.

Page 129:   "Far from being the final religious refinement": *Mir* 85.

Page 130:   Muddled arguments of Idealists: *SBJ* 210.

Page 130:   Idealists borrowings from other traditions: *PR* 131-32.

Page 131:   "The Pantheist's God does nothing": *Mir* 96.

Page 131:   "An impersonal God—well and good": *Mir* 96-97.

Page 131:   "As soon as he attempts seriously to live by Philosophy": *PR* 143.

Page 131:   "From Pantheism to Theism": *PR* 144.

Page 131:   "The Absolute was 'there,' ": *SBJ* 210.

Page 132:   Absolute "had much of the quality of Heaven": *SBJ* 211.

Page 132:   "Greatly impressed by the author's truthful antithesis": *AMR* 301.

Page 132:   Watching oneself undermines one's sense of sincerity: *SBJ* 61-62.

Page 133:   Mild form of dissociation: *AMR* 152.

Page 133:   Lewis enjoyed the process of writing: Havard, p. 221.

Page 133:   "Motive-scratching": *EL* 33.

Page 133:   Reminders of a deeper reality: *SBJ* 219-20.

Page 134:   "Christianity itself was very sensible": *SBJ* 223.

Page 134:   Christian authors versus non-Christian: *SBJ* 213-14.

Page 134:   Coghill "a thoroughgoing supernaturalist": *SBJ* 212.

Page 134:   "[Today I] was thinking": *AMR* 431-32.

Page 135:   "Holding something at bay": *SBJ* 224.

Page 135:   "Call his soul his own": *SBJ* 228.

Page 135:   "I suppose everyone knows this fear": *Per* 10.

Page 135:   "To avoid entanglements and interferences": *THS* 72.

Page 135:   "Our Lord does all things for each": *THS* 289.

Page 136:   "The smell of pews": *THS* 234.

Page 136:   "A kind of exhalation": *THS* 318.

Page 136:   "They had no picture in their minds": *THS* 318.

Page 136:   "A boundary had been crossed": *THS* 318-19.

Page 137:   "It was high time that she went in": *THS* 382.

Page 137:   "In the Trinity Term of 1929": *SBJ* 228-97.

Chapter 8: Finding Truth in the Old Beliefs

Page 139:   Dejected and reluctant convert: *SBJ* 228-29.

Page 139   "Theism, pure and simple, not to Christianity": *SBJ* 230.

Page 139:   Attending church as a gesture: *SBJ* 233.

Page 140:   Barfield says *conversion* isn't the right word: Barfield, p. 5.

Page 140:   Medieval model of human personality: *SL* 37.

Page 141:   The dispute over unpaid bills: *TST* 257-59.

Page 141:   "You have waited": *LP* 8:290.

Page 141:   Resentment at his own dependency: *LP* 6:133-34.

Page 142:   "My dear, dear Papy": *LRev* 267.

Page 142:   Albert said which stationery to use: *LRev* 269.

Page 142:   "Taking it like a hero": quoted in Wilson 112.

Page 142:   "All of a sudden, Jack saw": Wilson 112.

Page 143:   "Terrific *personality*": *LCSL* 138.

Page 143:   A snobbish element in his feelings toward his father: *LP* 5:330-31.

Page 143:   Annoyance with Albert's eccentricities: *SBJ* 160.

Page 144:   He had treated his father "abominably": *TST* 359.

Page 144:   No sin in his own life was worse: Hooper, p. 13.

Page 144:   Both brothers think of their mother's passing: Griffin, p. 56.

Page 144:   Memoirs of the Lewis Family: These volumes are now commonly re-ferred to as *The Lewis Papers.* The originals are in the Marion E. Wade Center at Wheaton College, with microfilm copies at the Bodleian Library in Oxford and the Southern Historical Collection in Chapel Hill, North Carolina.

Page 144:   "May I never forget that": *LP* 3:120.

Page 144:   Taking Communion to avoid a row: *SBJ* 161.

Page 145:   "We have come back to Puritania": *PR* 196.

Page 145:   "Finding more and more, the element of truth": *TST* 319-20.

Page 145:   "Picking & choosing": *TST* 330-31.

Page 145:   "That is another of the beauties" *TST* 333-34.

Page 145:   Things going well spiritually: *TST* 338.

Page 146:   "There seems to be no end to it": *TST* 338-39.

Page 146:   "Terrible things are happening to me": *LRev* 283-84.

Page 146:   Writing religious poetry of his own: *TST* 385.

Page 146:   "I have just passed on from believing in God": *TST* 425.

Page 147:   "Lies breathed through silver": *Mir* 139.

Page 147:   "A real though unfocused gleam of divine truth": *Mir* 139.

Page 147:   "Rum thing": *SBJ* 223-24.

Page 147:   Weldon was "determined to be a villain": *AMR* 483.

Page 147:   A "Christian 'of a sort' ": *AMR* 379.

Page 148:   "[This is] one of those rare works": *LCSL* 143.

Page 148:   "The very formula of reality": *Mir* 130.

Page 149:   Christ like a strong man or a diver: *Mir* 116, 1309.

Page 149:   Religious significance in the art of diving: *TST* 369.

Page 149:   "Throw yourself down safely": Kathryn Lindskoog, *Finding the Landlord* (Chicago: Cornerstone Press, 1995), p. 76.

Page 149:   "The cure of death is dying": *PR* 167.

Page 149:   John's symbolic baptism: *PR* 167-72.

Page 150:   "In his will is our peace": Lindskoog, p. 79.

Page 150:   Resolved the "dialectic of desire": *SBJ* 219.

Page 150:   "The naked Other": *SBJ* 221.

Page 150:   Christianity is a Way: *SBJ* 225.

Page 150:   "I know very well when, but hardly how": *SBJ* 237.

Page 151:   "Eden before the Fall": *LCSL* 154.

Page 152:   "Annihilating space": *SBJ* 157.

Page 152:   His apprehensions about riding on his brother's motorcycle: Sayer, p. 90.

Page 152:   "It was during that trip": Warren Lewis, *Biography,* p. 231.

Page 153:   This imaginative supposal about Lewis's ride to Whipsnade includes these phrases from his books: "silent, dewy, cobwebby hours of the morning": *LAL* 78; "Portraits of Christ": *Mir* 23-24; "True myth": *TST* 247; "The face above all worlds": *Per* 111. Other phrases in this passage taken from Lewis are discussed elsewhere in this book.

Epilogue

Page 155:   "Intellectual stagnation": *TST* 202.

Page 156: "The organ of meaning," "the organ of truth": *SLE* 265.

Page 156: Stability versus stagnation: *CR* 76; *SLE* 10.

Page 156: "Growth is the synthesis": *SLE* 105.

Page 156: "Never more beautiful since": *SBJ* 184.

Page 158: "I do not think that all who choose wrong roads": *GD* 6.

Page 158: Example of walking a dog: *TST* 463.

Page 159: "Only Supernaturalists really see Nature": *Mir* 67.

Page 159: "God never meant man": *MC* 659.

Page 160: Lewis's decreased introspection after his conversion: *SBJ* 233.

Page 160: "Spiritual megalomania": Barfield, pp. 24-25.

Page 160: "Ruthless, sleepless, unsmiling concentration on the self": *SL* ix.

Page 161: Quoted in Richard Waldheim, *F. H. Bradley* (Baltimore, Md.: Penguin, 1969), p. 24.

Page 162: Hooper's account of Lewis's vision: Walter Hooper, "C. S. Lewis: The Man and His Thought" in *Essays on C. S. Lewis and George MacDonald,* ed. Cynthia Marshall (Lewiston, N.Y.: Edwin Mellon, 1991), pp. 27-28.

Page 163: The desire to achieve greatness was an idol: *TST* 379-80.

Page 164: Sales of Lewis's books: Graham A. Cole, "C. S. Lewis: An Evangelical Appreciation," *The Reformed Theological Review* 53, no. 3 (1994): 102.

Page 164: "He was the most thoroughly converted man": Hooper "Reminiscences," p. 6.

Page 164: Memoir writers have noted: Lawlor, p. 3; Brewer, p. 64; Starr, p. 125; Coghill, p. 66; Schofield, p. 57.

Biographical Materials on C. S. Lewis

Baker, Leo. "Near the Beginning." In *"C. S. Lewis at the Breakfast Table" and Other Reminiscences.* Edited by James Como. New York: Macmillan, 1979.

Barfield, Owen. *Owen Barfield on C. S. Lewis.* Edited by G. B. Tennyson. Middletown, Conn.: Wesleyan University Press, 1989.

Brewer, Derek. "The Tutor: A Portrait." In *"C. S. Lewis at the Breakfast Table" and Other Reminiscences.* Edited by James Como. New York: Macmillan, 1979.

Carpenter, Humphrey. *The Inklings: C. S. Lewis, J. R. R. Tolkien, Charles Williams, and Their Friends.* Boston: Houghton Mifflin, 1979.

Christopher, Joe R. " 'From the Master's Lips': W. B. Yeats as C. S. Lewis Saw Him." *CSL: The Bulletin of the New York C. S. Lewis Society* 6, no. 1 (1974): 14-19.

Coghill, Neville. "The Approach to English." In *Light on C. S. Lewis.* Edited by Jocelyn Gibb. New York: Harcourt, Brace & World, 1965.

Como, James T., ed. *"C. S. Lewis at the Breakfast Table" and Other Reminiscences.* New York: Macmillan, 1979.

Dorsett, Lyle W. *And God Came In: The Extraordinary Story of Joy Davidman: Her Life and Marriage to C. S. Lewis.* New York: Macmillan, 1983.

Gardner, Helen. "Clive Staples Lewis, 1898-1963." *Proceedings of the British Academy* 51 (1965): 417-28.

Gibb, Jocelyn, ed. *Light on C. S. Lewis.* New York: Harcourt, Brace & World, 1965.

Gilbert, Douglas, and Clyde S. Kilby. *C. S. Lewis: Images of His World.*

Grand Rapids, Mich.: Eerdmans, 1973.

Green, Roger Lancelyn, and Walter Hooper. *C. S. Lewis: A Biography*. New York: Harcourt Brace Jovanovich, 1974.

Gresham, Douglas H. *Lenten Lands*. New York: Macmillan, 1988.

Griffin, William. *Clive Staples Lewis: A Dramatic Life*. New York: Harper & Row, 1986.

Hardie, Colin. "A Colleague's Note on C. S. Lewis." *Inklings—Jahrbuch fur Literatur und Asthetik* 3 (1985): 177-82.

Havard, Robert E. "Philia: Jack at Ease." In *"C. S. Lewis at the Breakfast Table" and Other Reminiscences*. Edited by James Como. New York: Macmillan, 1979.

Hooper, Walter. *C. S. Lewis: A Companion and Guide*. San Francisco: HarperSanFrancisco, 1996.

—————. "C. S. Lewis: The Man and His Thought." *Essays on C. S. Lewis and George MacDonald*. Edited by Cynthia Marshall. Lewiston, N.Y.: Edwin Mellon, 1991.

—————. "Reminiscences." *Mythlore* 12 (June 1976): 5-9.

—————. *Through Joy and Beyond: A Pictorial Biography of C. S. Lewis*. New York: Macmillan, 1982.

Keefe, Carolyn, ed. *C. S. Lewis: Speaker and Teacher*. Grand Rapids, Mich.: Zondervan, 1971.

Kilby, Clyde S., and Marjorie Lamp Mead. *Brothers and Friends: The Diaries of Major Warren Hamilton Lewis*. San Francisco: Harper & Row, 1982.

Lawlor, John. *C. S. Lewis: Memories and Reflections*. Dallas: Spence, 1998.

Lea, Kathleen. "Memories of C. S. Lewis as a Colleague." *The Chesterton Review* 17 (August 1991): 399-401.

Lewis, Warren H. *C. S. Lewis: A Biography*. Unpublished typescript available at the Marion E. Wade Center, Wheaton College, and the Bodleian Library in Oxford.

—————, ed. "The Lewis Papers: The Memoirs of the Lewis Family, 1850-1930." Oxford: Leeborough Press, 1933. 11 vols. Unpublished bound papers, Marion E. Wade Collection, Wheaton College, Wheaton, Illinois. Used by permission.

McGovern, Eugene. "Our Need for Such a Guide." In *"C. S. Lewis at the*

Breakfast Table" and Other Reminiscences. Edited by James Como. New York: Macmillan, 1979.

Milward, Peter. "A Jesuit Remembers C. S. Lewis." *The Chesterton Review* 17 (August 1991): 385-88.

Moynihan, Martin. "C. S. Lewis and T. D. Weldon." *Seven: An Anglo-American Literary Review* 5 (1984): 101-5.

Sayer, George. *Jack: C. S. Lewis and His Times.* San Francisco: Harper & Row, 1988.

Schofield, Stephen, ed. *In Search of C. S. Lewis.* South Plainfield, N.J.: Bridge, 1983.

Starr, Nathan C. "Good Cheer and Sustenance." In *"C. S. Lewis at the Breakfast Table" and Other Reminiscences.* Edited by James Como. New York: Macmillan, 1979.

Tennyson, G. B., ed. *Owen Barfield on C. S. Lewis.* Middletown, Conn.: Wesleyan University Press, 1989.

Vanauken, Sheldon. *A Severe Mercy.* New York: Harper & Row, 1977.

Wain, John. *Sprightly Running: Part of an Autobiography.* New York: St. Martin's, 1962.

Wilson, A. N. *C. S. Lewis: A Biography.* New York: W. W. Norton, 1990.

Index

Permissions & Acknowledgments

Sections in chapters one and two summarizing Lewis's childhood and boyhood are adapted from David C. Downing, Planets in Peril *(Amherst: University of Massachusetts Press, 1992). Used by permission.*

Some material in chapter two is adapted from David C. Downing, "From Ogre to Buffoon: Robert Capron in The Magician's Nephew," CSL: The Bulletin of the New York C. S. Lewis Society *31, no. 12 (2000): 1-6.*

Two paragraphs in chapter three are adapted from David C. Downing, "From Pillar to Postmodernism: C. S. Lewis and Current Critical Discourse," Christianity and Literature *46 (Winter 1997): 169-78.*

Sections of chapter four are adapted from David C. Downing, "The Dungeon of His Soul: Lewis's Unfinished 'Quest of Bleheris,' " Seven: An Anglo-American Literary Review *15 (1998): 37-54.*

Some material in chapter five is adapted from David C. Downing, "The Torch of Civilization: C. S. Lewis on War and Peace," The Canadian C. S. Lewis Journal *(Spring 1999): 13-21.*

Some paragraphs in chapter six are adapted from David C. Downing, "The Discarded Mage: Lewis the Scholar-Novelist on Merlin's Moral Taint," Christian Scholar's Review *27, no. 4 (1998): 406-15.*

The following extracts are reprinted by permission from the C. S. Lewis Company.

Surprised by Joy *by C. S. Lewis copyright © C. S. Lewis Pte. Ltd. 1955.*
They Stand Together *by C. S. Lewis copyright © C. S. Lewis Pte. Ltd. 1979.*
Miracles *by C. S. Lewis copyright © C. S. Lewis Pte. Ltd. 1947, 1960.*
Pilgrim's Regress *by C. S. Lewis copyright © C. S. Lewis Pte. Ltd. 1933.*
The Problem of Pain *by C. S. Lewis copyright © C. S. Lewis Pte. Ltd. 1940.*
Unpublished material by C. S. Lewis copyright © C. S. Lewis Pte. Ltd.

Photographs are used by permission of the Marion E. Wade Center, Wheaton College, Wheaton, Illinois.

J. R. R. Tolkien photograph used by permission of Houghton Mifflin.